Building Operational Excellence

IT Best Practices Series

This book is published as a part of the IT Best Practices Series—a collaboration between Intel Press and Addison-Wesley Professional, a division of Pearson Education. Books in this series focus on the information technology challenges companies face in today's dynamic, Internet-based, business environment, as well as on the opportunities to improve IT performance and thereby gain a competitive edge. Some of the books explain proven strategies to help business executives and managers develop needed capabilities. Other books show technical professionals exactly how to implement specific solutions. The series overall reflects Intel's Best Practices Program, developed with leading researchers, vendors, and end-users to meet the challenges and opportunities described. These Best Practices recognize that companies must be agile and adaptable in the face of diverse and rapidly changing technologies, and, in particular, must be prepared and able to integrate multivendor, e-Business tools. Thus, the theme of this series is: *Making it all work together*.

Books in this series include:

> *The Adaptive Enterprise:*
> *IT Infrastructure Strategies to Manage Change and Enable Growth*
> —Bruce Robertson and Valentin Sribar

> *Securing Business Information:*
> *Strategies to Protect the Enterprise and Its Network*
> —F. Christian Byrnes and Dale Kutnick

> *Enriching the Value Chain:*
> *Infrastructure Strategies Beyond the Enterprise*
> —Bruce Robertson and Valentin Sribar

> *Building Operational Excellence:*
> *IT People and Process Best Practices*
> —Bruce Allen and Dale Kutnick

For detailed information about these and other books, as well as announcements of forthcoming books in the series, visit the Intel Press and Addison-Wesley Professional Web sites:

www.intel.com/intelpress
www.awprofessional.com

Building Operational Excellence

IT People and Process Best Practices

Bruce Allen
Dale Kutnick

INTEL
PRESS

✦ Addison-Wesley
Pearson Education

Boston • San Francisco • New York • Toronto • Montreal
London • Munich • Paris • Madrid
Capetown • Sydney • Tokyo • Singapore • Mexico City

Pearson Education offers discounts on this book when ordered in quantity for special sales. For more information, please contact:

Pearson Education Corporate Sales Division
201 W. 103rd Street
Indianapolis, IN 46290
(800) 428-5331
corpsales@pearsoned.com

Library of Congress Cataloging-in-Publication Data

Allen, Bruce (Bruce R.)
   Building operational excellence : IT people and process best practices / Bruce Allen, Dale Kutnick.
      p. cm.
   Includes bibliographical references and index.
   ISBN 0-201-76737-6 (pbk. : alk. paper)
   1. Information resources management—Handbooks, manuals, etc. 2. Information technology—Management—Handbooks, manuals, etc. 3. Information technology—Evaluation—Handbooks, manuals, etc. I. Kutnick, Dale. II. Title.

T58.64 .A434 2002
658.4'038—dc21

                                                                    2002066532

For information on obtaining permission for use of material from this work, please submit a written request to:

Publisher, Intel Press
Intel Corporation
5200 NE Elam Young Parkway JF4-326
Hillsboro, OR 97124-6461
E-mail: intelpress@intel.com

ISBN 0-201-76737-6

Text printed on recycled paper

1 2 3 4 5 6 7 8 9 10—CRS—0605040302

First printing, May 2002

Contents

Preface

Enterprises today are concerned about two conflicting stresses placed on their IT departments by the incursion of the Web: the need for rapid adaptability to change, but which must be done in an environment that requires significantly higher levels of security and customer service. Although IT has always faced the concurrent challenges of responsiveness, security, and service, current conditions punish inferior performance in any of these areas so acutely that companies need to invest wisely in IT processes simply to remain in business.

Many books describe in great detail the application of technology to the problems confronting IT. Bookstore shelves creak with tomes on Web services, application servers, supply-chain integration, enterprise application integration, and related topics. But few books discuss how an IT organization—regardless of the specific technologies it deploys—can examine its own processes and improve them. The titles in the Best Practices series present IT best practices in numerous important fields of endeavor: security, infrastructure design, e-Business integration, and several other IT disciplines. These books discuss the problems without tying the solutions to specific technologies. They guide you to solve problems rather than to implement specific technology solutions.

This book focuses specifically on how an IT organization can assess its own operational processes and bring them to the level of best practices—or operations excellence. It is based on the proposition that today excellence in operations is a strategic competitive advantage. The recommendations made in this volume are derived from the work and experiences of META Group analysts within numerous IT organizations throughout the world. The information is presented in a sequenced series of steps that invariably define a goal, measure the current state, and establish a path for filling the gaps between the current state and the articulated goal.

Every step within this process requires you to spend considerable time identifying the form the goal should take so that best practices are implemented in a thoughtful manner, leading to faster response, lower costs, and improved quality of services.

For Whom Is This Book Intended?

This book is intended for IT managers who are highly motivated to improve the quality, timeliness, or economy of the operational services they provide. These managers are working in IT departments of at least several dozen employees and possibly several hundred. The department must be large enough that concern about internal processes occupies an important place in the design and implementation of new projects. Sites that run on an ad hoc basis, or that view processes as unnecessary encumbrances, may benefit from this book, but their lack of context for many of the issues discussed here will diminish the profit they could derive from its suggestions. Sites with more than several hundred IT employees will need to apply the recommendations with a finer granularity than smaller sites. The book discusses how to do this effectively at several junctures where it is particularly appropriate.

The primary focus of this book is the establishment of excellence for IT operations. The term *operations* refers to the collection of tasks and processes traditionally involved in running the computing infrastructure. Due to its highly specific nature, best practices in security are not discussed. A companion book in this series, *Securing Business Information*, presents in considerable detail the implementation of best practices in enterprise security; it should be consulted for information in this area.

This book also does not cover the areas of application development and maintenance, infrastructure design, or project management. These special disciplines have unique requirements that warrant specific techniques for advancing their quality, timeliness, and economy. Hence, they are treated elsewhere in books, materials, and resources available from Intel Press and other publishers.

The Elevator Pitch

This book is about optimizing IT operations.

■ IT operations comprise dozens, sometimes hundreds, of tasks. These tasks, when properly sequenced, are the building blocks of IT processes. For example, an IT process, such as storage allocation for a database, is made up of numerous tasks that involve the database, the operating system, the storage-management software, and the physical storage devices or network.

■ Processes are often viewed as independent activities, each having unique characteristics. Because of this, at sites that are not employing best practices, processes are automated infrequently, rarely quantified, and even more rarely documented; as a result, they are prone to error.

To achieve best practices in IT operations, processes are catalogued, compared to the way in which similar processes have been designed and implemented by experts at sites that have attained the best possible level of operations. IT managers are encouraged to construct inventory of the gaps between current and best practices.

The next step is to fill the gaps. Several steps are involved in this process, as the gaps to fill are selected on the basis of site-specific factors such as cost, priority, degree of support within the organization, and other pressures. This book discusses gap analysis and prioritization of filling gaps in considerable detail. Most IT organizations will benefit from these analyses.

Some organizations may press further if they have the mandate to make larger-scale changes in the pursuit of best practices. The additional steps they would pursue rest on the observation that processes in different, but related, fields of activity often share similar goals and requirements. These processes can be grouped into a common set that can be subjected to best practices.

These sets of processes are called centers of excellence (or COEs). This book shows readers how to aggregate processes into COEs and how to use the concept of COEs to implement best practices. When properly done, COEs:

■ Optimize efficiency and effectiveness among all processes

■ Integrate like tasks and processes

■ Leverage automation

- Ensure clear accountability
- Provide multi-platform support
- Directly correlate to service-level agreements
- Roll up more easily to cost centers
- Provide consistent customer experience

In addition, COEs enable metrics to be applied easily and consistently to tasks so that targets for further improvement can be identified.

To show you how to create COEs within the IT organization, and how to use COEs to improve services, this book identifies a progression of steps, each of which receives a full chapter:

- Chapter 1 explains what the term best practices means in general and in IT specifically.
- Chapter 2 defines the fundamental units, the task and the process.
- Chapter 3 explains how to perform gap analyses and refine processes.
- Chapter 4 tells you what COEs are and how they can be built from processes.
- Chapter 5 explains how to apply metrics to improved processes and to COEs.
- Chapter 6 tells you how to derive the maximum benefit from the adoption of IT best practices. This discussion includes marketing IT services within the enterprise, pricing those services, and providing them with the reliability consistent with service-level agreements.
- Chapter 7 is a catalog of the most common IT processes. This reference includes information on the constituent tasks, the best practices for that process, and metrics to use in monitoring quality of implementation.
- Chapter 8 is a catalog for COEs.

Readers who take the time to go through this book attentively will understand how to implement best IT practices within their organization regardless of the company's structure or unique IT exigencies.

Getting the Most Out of This Book

Like all volumes in the IT Best Practices series, this book is intended for immediate use. The book's style and approach are designed to make it useful in solving difficult problems in a practical manner. To this end, many forms that the reader may find helpful in implementing specific steps are provided, and readers should feel free to copy these forms and adapt them for their specific situations.

This is a hands-on book. Because of its practical nature, the book does not require sequential reading, although this is the preferred approach. Chapters on various concepts and processes can be read independently. Although later concepts do build on ones presented earlier, nothing should discourage the reader from flipping forward to chapters of particular interest. However, the authors strongly recommend that before implementation is undertaken, a complete reading of the relevant sections should be done so that all steps are performed in the right order and in the right manner.

The Appendix that follows the core presentation provides useful reference material, including pointers to other books and a Web site that the reader may find helpful, and a glossary of important terms.

Note

> Due to the cumbersomeness of the phrase "he or she" and the awkwardness of "s/he," this book uses the generic form of "he" to refer to positions or persons whose gender is immaterial to the topic. The authors recognize that, in many enterprises, the roles and positions under discussion are filled by both women and men.

Acknowledgments

The authors wish to thank the many people who helped make this book possible. Brian Hellauer and Donna MacIver of the META Group did a wonderful job of tracking down research material and stitching it together so that it could be used to best advantage. Andrew Binstock, of Pacific Data Works, contributed technology analysis that was the key to giving the book its current quality. Without their help, there would be no book. Any errors that remain, of course, are entirely our own.

As with most published works, editors are invisible even though their contributions appear on every page. David B. Spencer, of Intel Corporation, cleaned, tightened, and sharpened the manuscript.

Adam Bianci provided support and feedback during the writing of this book. Fergus O'Scannlain, Jonathan Birck, and Rich Burton validated the content of the book's usefulness and accuracy and provided valuable feedback.

Rich Bowles, Dan Fineberg, and Eric Heerwagen, all of Intel Corporation, especially must be thanked for their contributions in putting together this series of IT Best Practices books and sponsoring it under the Intel Press imprint. We are honored to participate in this program.

Finally, thanks to our families and colleagues whose patience as we worked on the manuscript was quietly and deeply appreciated.

—Bruce Allen
 Vice President META Group

—Dale Kutnick
 Chairman of META Group

Chapter 1

What Are IT Best Practices?

Because of the rapid advance of the Web into corporate business cycles, many companies must reconsider the role played by Information Technology (IT) operations. Operations are the collection of tasks and processes involved in designing, implementing, and maintaining the corporate computing infrastructure. By demanding that companies respond immediately to change and deliver impeccable customer support, customers forced IT management to recognize operations as a strategic part of a successful customer experience.

Today, IT managers must design operations for great agility and flexibility, and those operations must perform the old tasks flawlessly. Prior to assuming this new role in the IT hierarchy, operations experienced little change; that change occurred slowly and only after extended planning.

For IT operations to assume their correct place as a strategic business advantage, IT managers must be sure that their operations run correctly. Correctly here means in the best possible manner; it does not mean good enough to satisfy the immediate needs. This distinction is important and not obvious. Good enough for the current needs is a level of performance that is acceptable only if the current needs remain static. However, when operations staff must respond to change quickly, they cannot be handcuffed by static policies. They need a higher standard that targets the best possible way of doing things. Thus, as needs change, operations staff, technicians, programmers, and administrators can respond with minimum disruption.

An excellent analogy exists in the field of software development. Following the so-called "quick and dirty" method, programs are written to run only an immediate task. So, they handle the current needs but often require a complete rewrite if the needs change. Good programming practices suggest that the criterion to assess the quality of a programming process is not whether the programs fill customer needs (this result is assumed!), but whether the program's development follows standardized engineering methodology. This criterion applies to how it was designed, coded, debugged, and tested. With this knowledge, an outsider can tell the quality of the program. By following best practices for design, coding, testing, and so forth, a site can rely with confidence on the programs it uses and the ability to adapt these programs as needed. Sites that improve their IT operations in a comparable way can enjoy similar benefits.

Obstacles to Improving IT Operations

For enhanced IT operations to achieve their strategic importance, an enterprise frequently encounters several immediate obstacles, depending on the site. This chapter addresses the challenges individually by presenting techniques discussed later in more detail. To appreciate these techniques, however, first the obstacles to improving IT operations must be spelled out.

The initial problem to solve is a lack of inventory of operations tasks. IT operations generally grow organically, rather than as a function of deliberate planning. For example, when administrators install an application server, they can foresee certain operations and prescribe their execution. However, over time the managers and administrators will discover problems that require special handling, and they will develop a work-around. These work-arounds are rarely inventoried, and they exist only as an oral tradition within the department. Consequently, it is difficult for managers to know exactly which tasks are performed at a site, much less an enterprise.

Lack of documentation for operational tasks is the second obstacle to address. The best-documented sites often have extensive records of the written policies but precious little documentation of the actual implementation. In fact, most departments are unable to produce a current network diagram. That omission, which is generally a function of limited time rather than lack of care, means crucial knowledge about operations is retained only in the memory of specific administrators and managers. Inevitably, the company is at risk if a problem occurs and the one person with the information is unavailable. This situation represents an obstacle to operations excellence because it is impossible to improve tasks that cannot be documented.

The third obstacle is the large number and wide variety of tasks. Administrators and operators perform dozens, sometimes hundreds, of small tasks that vary in complexity and importance, each of which is unique but yet similar to other functions. As a result, sites have difficulty establishing best practices for operations, because doing so would create hundreds of policies, one for every discrete task that an operator might be called upon to perform. This obstacle is specifically addressed in the chapters that follow.

The final obstacle, a tendency to one-off solutions, derives from the place in the hierarchy traditionally assigned to operations. The operations department was often designed and run according to the concept of performing a variety of tasks well enough to meet the immediate need. Time spent elaborating a solution that exceeded the current needs was frowned upon as time wasted. Notice, for example, that Perl, the scripting language used for many administrative tasks, for many years was lauded for the ease with which it enabled operators and administrators to write quick and dirty, one-off scripts that could be thrown away. The use of one-off scripts emphasizes expediency to the detriment of quality, and it fosters a "just get it done" attitude that is invariably an obstacle to any quality improvement campaign.

Later in this chapter, the section entitled "The Three Fundamental Steps" explains how a thoughtful implementation of best practices addresses these four obstacles.

What Do Best Practices Mean and Why Are They Important?

A best practice is a term of art. It has been used in discussing quality improvement at corporations for many years. In its original sense, the term referred to best practices known in the industry. For example, if your hotel implements the level of service found at the Ritz-Carlton hotel chain, you would be adopting a best practice, as you would by achieving the reliability of Federal Express in your messenger service. In this sense, best practices required considerable research into the techniques used by market leaders. This definition, however, quickly ran into two contradictions/difficulties:

■ These best practices were not useful to all companies in an industry. For example, hotels whose differentiator is low cost cannot provide the level of service of a Ritz-Carlton and have little desire to do so. Hence, measuring their service orientation against the Ritz-Carlton was hardly a productive exercise. To be useful, best practices had to be modified to reflect the specific mission and capabilities of the existing company, rather than the mission of leading exponents in the larger industry.

■ Many market leaders viewed their expertise as a competitive advantage. They were not willing to share information about how they achieved unique or optimal performance, unless the bar to entry was so high that releasing that information was unlikely to assist competitors. In some industries, such as the hotel industry, the information could not be controlled easily. But in industries where IT organizations implemented best practices, the need for secrecy was extremely high. And, many companies considered information about the specific technologies that they used a trade secret.

Over time, then, two things became clear. First, consultants and others who work at a wide variety of firms are in a position to see who does what things well. They are in the best position to know best practices. Their exposure to many different IT organizations gives them a unique breadth of perspective that IT managers would find difficult to acquire. Second, administrators need to develop and implement best practices according to the needs of their enterprise. What makes best practices best is that they work optimally for a given site.

As a result, this book is based on material derived from work that IT consultancy META Group did in conjunction with Intel Corporation. With it, companies can establish specific best practices for their own sites, and they can design, develop, and implement these best practices with a minimum of disruption.

Better Practices versus Best Practices

Companies looking to improve their operations often are questing for better operations. For example, a company that wants better tape management might do research and purchase a tape-management package, send an operator off for training, migrate to the package, and document the new procedures. If the software is better than the existing tape-management solution, this series of steps will lead to a better practice. It will not, however, lead to a best practice. Best practices are long-term commitments: They involve up-front analysis, thoughtful implementation, establishment of metrics for quantifying success in the stated operations, and a commitment to use the metrics as input to a continuous cycle of improvement.

Early studies of processes for the purpose of improvement occurred in the field of software development. Until the advent of process management in programming, "cowboys" developed software. These talented programmers worked by themselves and banged out huge amounts of code. Generally, they were difficult to manage: They did not follow shop standards for coding, were not interested in validating the software beyond simple tests, were not amenable to helping in debugging, and provided little or no documentation. They survived into the mid-1980s because of their talent. But by the mid-1980s, programs had become too complex for a single programmer to be effective. As a result, many development sites had to adopt the techniques of team programming. While that solved the cowboy-induced problems, the move to team programming introduced a whole series of new difficulties when software cycles became longer and quality continued to suffer. New frameworks of best practices appeared to handle the problem. After some false starts, several models of best practices emerged, such as the *Capability Maturity Model (CMM)* from Carnegie-Mellon University's Software Engineering Institute (SEI), listed in Appendix A. Table 1.1, whose definitions are taken from SEI literature, explains the five levels of maturity in CMM.

As Table 1.1 shows, "cowboy programming" is a synonym for the initial maturity stage. An attempt at better practices can move development organization from level 1 to level 2 or from level 2 to level 3. However, to reach levels 4 and 5, the required steps entail a complete revamping of the software development process. Reaching those levels requires best practices; better practices that do not involve wholesale systemic improvement will be insufficient.

What, then, are the core features of best practices? Those practices must be process-oriented, applicable to the current situation, repeatable, documented, and measurable. In this book, any claim to best practices requires the following elements.

1. Best practices require a *process orientation*, which forces a company to see its internal activities as processes rather than as a sequence of isolated tasks. By viewing activities as processes rather

Table 1.1 The Five Maturity Levels of Software Development in the CMM Model

Least Mature	1. Initial	The software process is characterized as ad hoc and occasionally even chaotic. Few processes are defined, and success depends on individual effort and heroics.
	2. Repeatable	Basic project management processes are established to track cost, schedule, and functionality. The necessary process discipline is in place to repeat earlier successes on projects with similar applications.
⇑ ⇓	3. Defined	The software process for both management and engineering activities is documented, standardized, and integrated into a standard software process for the organization. All projects use an approved, tailored version of the organization's standard software process for developing and maintaining software.
	4. Managed	Detailed measures of the software process and product quality are collected. Both the software process and products are quantitatively understood and controlled.
Most Mature	5. Optimized	Continuous process improvement is enabled by quantitative feedback from the process and from piloting innovative ideas and technologies.

than tasks, a company can apply policies and seek improvements that will enhance all the tasks within a specific process. Therefore, the CMM maturity levels in Table 1.1 do not mention tasks, always referring to processes instead. For example, no level explicitly specifies how code should be written or tests should be scripted. Rather, the maturity levels specify the degree to which these processes must be standardized, documented, and so on. This process orientation is a higher level of abstraction and much more amenable to analysis for the purpose of quality improvement.

2. Best practices must reflect *the most highly regarded practices applicable* to the current company's situation and needs. As discussed previously, finding out how other companies have improved their processes can be difficult. And if the target com-

pany is not a direct match, the results of the research can be of little value. So, it behooves companies to perform an introspective vein of research in establishing their best practices. Numerous books are available on various best practices, although remarkably few are available on IT operations. However, by application of the steps described in the rest of this book, an IT group can develop its own best practice notions.

3. Best practices are *repeatable*. True best practices are codified (see the documentation element) and can be duplicated by other branches of the company or other sites on the basis of the experience of a single implementation. For example, if documentation is a best practice, the form that the documentation takes, the means by which it is created, and the persons who are in charge of its creation should be detailed in writing. In addition, sites need to establish metrics for measuring documentation results. Between the process specification and the metrics, any other department within the company that needs to establish documentation as part of its processes should be able to do so. If a process is not repeatable, it is likely to be a one-off solution and therefore outside the purview of best practices.

4. Best practices are *documented*. This key element is critical to the success of best practices. Sites that are not committed to documenting their processes are not ready to implement best practices.

5. Best practices define *metrics* to measure their effects. For best practices to be "best," some measure of their impact needs to be ascertained. Metrics have four principal purposes:

   - Metrics quantify the improvement gained through best practices. Knowing this score has several advantages. It enables the company to establish the return on investment (ROI) for its investment in best practices, and it helps the in-house champions of best practices to market their ideas better to the rest of the company. This last point is important. The implementation of best practices is inherently disruptive and has costs associated with it; as a result, it is frequently opposed by a variety of parties within the company. To dispel such opposition, advocates of best practices need to have data on the savings and benefits of each implementation so they are able to argue effectively for further best practices.

   - An equally important benefit of metrics is the information that they provide for improving the implementation of best practices. Activities and processes change over time, and best practices must change with them. Sometimes the nature of the change is so gradual that managers do not update best practices as the processes evolve. Metrics will make this problem visible because an out-of-date solution appears in the metrics numbers. An alert manager should see a pattern and inquire into the problem.

- Additionally, metrics establish a baseline for measuring refinements to processes. The benefits and ROI of a new policy can be gauged accurately if the metrics obtained for it have a rich base of historical data for before-and-after comparisons. By this comparison, the value and benefit of improvements can be gauged with accuracy.

- An IT organization must quantify the quality of its offerings if it provides services to other departments on a charge-back basis. Often the expected quality of service is formalized in a service level agreement (SLA). Proper metrics help an IT organization monitor compliance with the accepted SLAs.

Metrics also help shape tight definitions of best practices. Because each best practice must generate one or more metrics by which to measure success, best practices must be defined with specific quantifiable aspects. The key word here is "specific." All too commonly, managers design a detailed process that is poorly defined, that is, it has no quantifiable aspect to the benefit. The design is incomplete because the description contains no specific goals that the process will meet. If the design can state specific goals, it also can measure specific aspects. This requirement holds true even in areas that are normally not quantified.

In IT operations, clear detailed metrics are almost always definable. Their absence should be viewed as a flag pointing to poor design.

Chapter 7 of this book contains a catalog of IT operations, including the best practices that can be applied to them and the corresponding metrics to use. Although the material in Chapter 7 is a summary of concepts developed in the following chapters, you should see in the listed items the very specific nature of the data captured in the metrics. You should strive for this kind of specificity in your own best practices.

Stage 5 in Table 1.1, the last and highest stage in process improvement, focuses on metrics. Note that metrics enable level-5 maturity by pointing to places for further enhancement while measuring the benefits of new pilot projects and innovative ideas.

A commitment to constant improvement is required. CMM requires this commitment in stage 5. Likewise, Total Quality Management (TQM) and the Seven Habits series both require a self-perpetuating process of constant quality improvement.

This requirement is imposed for two reasons:

- A single, one-time fix cannot improve quality on a permanent basis. A single, directed solution might fix isolated quality problems, but best practices involve more than this limited target. Rather, they seek to improve all processes within a given discipline. Hence, one-time fixes will not work. Process improvement is an ongoing and constant commitment.

- Processes change and best practices must change with them. If quality improvement is not a sustained activity, best practices will slowly become ineffective as processes evolve. For example, in the days when mainframes ruled, tape management was a different discipline than it is today. Even though the basic goals might be similar—secure backups are kept up-to-date, for example—the volume of tapes and the way they are stored, inventoried, and handled have all changed. If a continuous commitment to quality is not implemented, the best practices from mainframe days might still be used for today's sites—leading to sub-optimal results.

These five elements and the commitment to constant improvement characterize all best practices and their implementations.

The Three Fundamental Steps

This book provides IT groups with a method for improving their operations by the application of best practices to numerous processes. The methodology relies in part on a three-step process. These steps are common to many quality improvement programs, and they are not inherently a function of IT operations. Companies installing best practices in divisions outside IT might well use the same three steps, although the details of the specific implementation would differ.

The three steps are:

1. Determine the current state.

2. Define the quality goal.

3. Determine the gaps between the current state and the goal, then implement best practices to fill these gaps.

At first glance, you might feel that these steps heavily favor analysis and planning over pure best-practices implementation. And indeed, that bias is real. The most difficult part of best-practices implementation lies in not identifying what the best practice is for a given endeavor, but in how to apply it and many other best practices into a cohesive web of quality commitments that raises IT operations to the level of excellence.

The process catalog in Chapter 7 has done some of the necessary legwork for ascertaining the best practices for specific processes, as it provides suggestions that will be valuable to many IT groups. In addition, that catalog of IT operations provides the corresponding metrics. However, this book would be of little value if it provided only this process catalog because a successful implementation of best practices requires that all quality gaps be filled consistently and that all processes meet a minimum level of quality. For example, one gains little from providing best practices for tape management at a site if the backup is performed in a haphazard, irregular manner.

To fill the gaps and ensure a minimum level of process quality, administrators must perform considerable analysis and planning before implementing a single best practice.

This book assists in assuring a comprehensive solution by grouping the gaps into cohesive wholes as a derivative benefit of grouping the processes themselves into *centers of excellence* (COEs). Gaps within one COE (that is, among multiple processes) can be addressed together. In this way, an IT organization can be certain a comprehensive solution has been implemented, rather than one that is incomplete because an unrelated gap unwittingly compromises the integrity of the solution.

Another book in this series, *Securing Business Information*, describes the implementation of best practices for enterprise security. It uses the same three steps in designing and implementing a comprehensive security policy. The same careful planning and analysis are performed before a strategy for implementation is formulated. The universality of the three-step process derives from its soundness. If performed properly, the three steps should lead an IT organization to the right decisions in improving its operations.

Other Benefits of the Three Fundamental Steps

Often, the simple performance of the individual steps contributes materially to quality improvement. For example, the first step requires the compilation of an *inventory of current processes*. This compilation, known as a baseline, is an inherently productive activity for an IT organization. By diligent execution of this step, IT managers have a complete list of all actions performed by all operators and administrators. Such a list is often an eye-opener. It exposes gaping holes, policy violations, and ineffective procedures, and it brings to light managers' incorrect perceptions of what their staffs are doing. The salutary benefit of this process is hard to overestimate. Moreover, it removes two key obstacles to best practices described earlier: a lack of an inventory of activities and a lack of documentation.

The second step requires the generation of a *quality goal*. This step in itself helps clarify objectives and priorities. As is discussed in future chapters, these goals need to be specific. By composing a document in which every goal is articulated, managers become more capable of directing their organizations and of making decisions that are consistent with an overarching framework.

The third step, *gap analysis*, requires managers to state where their current baseline falls short of the goal. This activity has great importance, as it will often reveal unsuspected areas of weakness. If you find a concentration of gaps in one area, subject it to further scrutiny before applying a remedy. When managers do not perform the gap analysis, they run the risk of applying an incomplete or incorrect solution. They are likely to correct one problem without recognizing that it is part of a larger gap, and that gap must be addressed completely or not at all.

The Area of Application

IT departments vary tremendously in their organization and responsibilities. In all companies, they provide operational support for computing. In most firms, they provide numerous other services—some involve charge-backs and SLAs with various departments, and some are provided on an as-is basis at no charged cost.

Notice that several disciplines are not covered. Applications development or maintenance and architecture have their own defined best practices as evidenced by CMM (see Table 1.1). Similarly, program management also has its own set of protocols for best practices that are distinctly outside the area of IT operations.

This chapter has explained in detail the theory and components of best practices and the problems that an organization is likely to encounter when implementing them. Chapter 2 begins the process of explaining the building blocks of implementation: the concepts of tasks and processes.

Chapter 2

Laying the Foundation

As explained in the previous chapter, the pursuit of best practices presupposes a migration to process-based IT operations. Treating operational tasks as part of a larger process allows IT departments to integrate them properly and to raise these tasks collectively to best-practice levels, rather than individually to different levels of excellence.

Defining Tasks and Processes

A task is a piece of work assigned to a person. Tasks can range from a simple action to complex and interrelated transactions. A process is a particular method of doing something that involves one or more tasks. Almost invariably, processes are defined in terms of their objectives while tasks are generally defined in terms of the nature of their activity. For example, storage management is an objective, but tape retrieval is a task. However, the purpose of a task and the means by which it is measured and assessed are always defined in the context of a process. The task of tape retrieval, for example, could be a task that occurs in several different processes, such as backup and tape management.

Tasks frequently can be divided into smaller units of work. For example, tape retrieval might involve vault access, tape-inventory access, secure transportation, and so forth. Each of these steps is also a task in itself. Exactly where to draw the line to determine what constitutes a task depends on the nature of the company's operations and its business. The level of granularity for a task constitutes a major issue in defining tasks and processes at a particular site. The following prosaic example demonstrates how the company's business and operations affect the granularity of task definition.

Suppose the task is mowing a large lawn with a tractor mower. At its most detailed level, this involves going to the mower shed, checking the mower for gasoline, attaching the collection bag, starting the mower, riding to the lawn, and so forth. This task could very easily include 20 or more different steps.

Suppose a Fortune 500 firm was revamping all of its operations. Where would mowing the lawn at corporate headquarters fit? Because the company employs a full-time gardener, this question is relevant. However, lawn mowing is not likely to appear anywhere. At best, "gardening" might appear as a task under the "housekeeping" process. But lawn mowing does not and should not appear anywhere.

Now suppose that the company's business is tending to public parks and gardens. In this case, mowing lawns certainly would be a task and could well be a process unto itself.

Finally, if the company's job were tending golf courses, where lawn mowing and tending are critical to the success of the business, mowing could be a process with specific tasks defined underneath it.

In each case, the work and the tools are very much the same, but the role that the work plays in the company's business and operations decides how that task is defined.

Hence, someone well versed both in IT operations and the business of the company or division should identify tasks and processes. Misalignment between a company's business needs and the IT group's priorities is an established recipe for disaster.

Consolidating Tasks into Processes

Processes, as mentioned previously, are a set of related tasks. Tasks are consolidated into processes in two ways.

Serialized Tasks

Processes in which tasks must be performed in a specific order fit in this category. Some processes, such as job scheduling and infrastructure planning, comprise serialized tasks. These processes are easy to document quickly. Participants generally can explain the whole process, their role in it, and what other participants do. They are a good place to start when creating an inventory of tasks.

Related Tasks

Most processes consist of a group of related tasks. These tasks need not be performed in a predefined order. Even though one task might depend on the prior execution of another, not all the tasks are part of a sequence. Disk storage management is a process that consists of related tasks. It includes file placement, archiving, backup–recovery, and numerous other tasks that often are performed independent of other tasks. Other compelling examples include contractor management, problem management, and many other processes, as listed in Table 2.1. Chapter 7 lists nearly 100 processes and the tasks they comprise.

Other Aspects of Tasks

Knowing what kinds of tasks compose a process becomes important later on. Serialized tasks use different metrics and have different repeatability characteristics than do related but independent tasks.

Another important aspect is identifying whether a task is automated or performed manually. When processes are first introduced into an organization, they generally require manual operation. As processes become stable commodities in the way that backup has, they introduce opportunities for automation. Automation and integration trigger stepwise process improvements. Notice that after each cycle of automation was followed by integration, the process improved. This improvement is established through metrics. As a result, the amount of possible improvement remaining is diminished. By assessing the level of automation and integration of a process, implementers of best practices can determine where best to allocate their investment and efforts.

The more mature a process is, the closer it comes to attaining best practices for that specific process. Highly automated and integrated processes are the goal of most quality-improvement efforts. Once achieved, their nemesis is change. Change, while inevitable, generally means a setback: The new process is less mature—maybe it requires more manual intervention and is less automated—and possibly it is less integrated with other processes. As a result, later discussions focus on making processes amenable to change in ways that reduce these effects.

From Tasks to Processes

A good place to start in identifying processes and constituent tasks is to examine the list of 38 processes in Table 2.1. This list occupies a central place in this discussion. It presents the key processes found in many businesses today. Clearly, not all businesses use every one of these processes, but large corporations will use most of them. In addition, every company has other processes not listed in this table that are unique to its business or to its way of doing things.

Take one of the processes on the list that corresponds to a process in your company. Then make a list of the tasks that constitute the process. After you have your list, make a guess on a scale of 1 to 10 as to how stable/mature the process is and how automated it is. After you have done so, compare your results with those shown for that procedure in the process catalog in Chapter 7. From this, you will get some sense of the types of tasks to include.

The processes presented in Chapter 7 probably look different from what you come up with. The various parts of each entry in the process catalog are summarized at the beginning of the chapter. Most are not needed for this initial exercise; only the list of tasks is important here. The next section enters more deeply into the layout and construction of this catalog.

Here's the important point: The tasks that you listed need to be roughly at the same level of granularity as those in the catalog. Only if your firm has special needs should the granularity be higher or lower. However, the granularity differs for small firms because they generally don't need to perform all the steps found in the processes of large enterprises.

Identify and Catalog Processes

The next major step is to define and catalog the processes that exist within the organization using the new taxonomy of tasks and processes.

Table 2.1 lists the 38 generic IT processes and operations on which we will focus during the following discussion, although, as you know, we could choose from many more processes. However, it is important to note that most business have fewer than 40 processes. A rule of thumb on these matters states that most mid-to-large enterprises have 100 or more tasks that can be aggregated into about 30 to 40 processes. If the company chooses to implement centers of excellence, then these 30 to 40 processes can be integrated into 5 to 10 centers of excellence.

Table 2.1 A Summary Process Catalog

Processes	
Application optimization	Negotiation management
Asset management	Network monitoring
Budget management	Output management
Business continuity	Performance management
Business relationship management	Physical database management
Capacity management	Problem management
Change management	Production acceptance
Configuration management	Production control
Contract management	Quality assurance
Contractor management	Security management
Cost recovery management	Service-level management
Database administration (physical)	Service-level agreement management
Disk storage management	Service request management
Facilities management	Software distribution
Hardware support	Software management
Infrastructure planning	Systems monitoring
Inventory management	Tape management
Job scheduling	Test lab management
Middleware management	Workload monitoring

Processes may be organized or structured different from what is shown here. Such differences are not a problem; the goal is to identify, at a fairly high level, what the organization's processes are.

Process Attributes

A standard list of process attributes forces definition of the key variables and implicitly answers the key questions of "what, who, when, and why." This list mirrors the attributes presented in the process catalog in Chapter 7.

The workflow, however, is just the surface of a process. The process template, even though it covers processes at a high level, defines a several other variables as well.

Process Name/Description

Name the process, using one of the examples from the catalog or something more specific or suitable to your site.

Automation

As mentioned, the level of automation within a process and its stability are key indicators of how much additional efficiency can be wrung from a given process. This scale (1=manual 10=automated) indicates the current automation level of a process.

Stability

This scale (1=dynamic 10= stable) indicates the current stability level of a process.

Purpose

The defined purpose of each process should reflect the organization's IT requirements.

Skills

Particular skills are needed by the staff to do the work satisfactorily. Only unique skills are listed. Occasionally, standard skills, such as attention to detail, are included because of their importance to the specific process.

Tasks

These tasks make up the process. This list is representative of large IT organizations. Your company could have different tasks depending on specific needs of the business.

Staffing

This item includes overall staff requirements, along with particular specialized job titles that are required.

Automation Technology

This item comprises the available applications or solutions that automate either tasks or the entire process.

Best Practices

The current and future techniques or activities utilized by IT leaders within this process constitute the best practices.

Metrics

These generally accepted or specialized measurements help define the results of the process, both internally (process efficiency) and externally (process effectiveness). Metrics also include specific measurements regarding the quantity and quality of changes made to the process.

Cross-Process Integration

This variable defines the tasks, skills, automation, and so forth that may be utilized in common by more than one application.

Futures

Futures refer to potential or imminent developments that must be considered when implementing best practices for this process.

Questions to Ask

These questions are useful to pose when gathering task and process information.

- What are the key processes for operations?
  - Are the key processes well defined, including workflows, process integration, automation, and skills?
  - Are the operational processes integrated across platforms?
  - What tools are available to maximize process performance?
- Does the organization favor stovepipe applications based on platforms?
  - Are resources allocated to evaluate and improve processes?
  - Are metrics in place to evaluate process performance?
  - Which processes need the most work?
  - Which processes need to be worked on first?

Asking these provocative questions can raise many issues. Defining a complete process catalog is not easy. More processes exist than most IT groups realize. No hard and fast rules distinguish between processes and sub-processes, define process importance, understand process interrelationships, or determine how changes in one might affect the others.

The key is to identify the level of detail that offers the greatest utility to the organization when included within the process catalog. An organization could have enough information to create a series of 50-page documents that cover process definition, process improvements, or process changes. Likewise, the organization could create complex spreadsheets and flowcharts that identify process flows, cross-process integration, and responsibility handoffs. This level of detail might be appropriate if the operations organization is large and highly centralized.

However, if the operations group is a smaller or more distributed, the process catalog should cover the variables at a somewhat less detailed level. In this situation, the process catalog should contain general process descriptions using the variables described here.

The catalog entries identify overall process policies and goals. A specific instance of a process within a particular area of operations may vary somewhat from the overall process task flow. This variance allows for some nuances in the way certain groups handle a particular task. Nevertheless, the catalog provides the model for how processes should be conducted.

Template Tools

How does an organization capture the information and disseminate the process catalog? Generally, operations organizations use tried-and-true office automation tools to generate documents and spreadsheets that they use to get the word out. Some use drawing tools and relational databases to document workflows and cross-process integration (see Figure 2.1), but such tools are not necessary.

After the organization addresses the issues regarding the scope of the catalog and captures the relevant information in a format everyone can use, the refined process catalog becomes unique to that organization.

Evaluate and Prioritize Processes

The process modeling techniques provided here offer snapshot views of operational performance related to an organization's goals, business drivers, processes, centers of excellence, and so forth. The outcome is an objective view of those processes that are most mature, those that need work, and those that can have the largest impact on the organization and the customer.

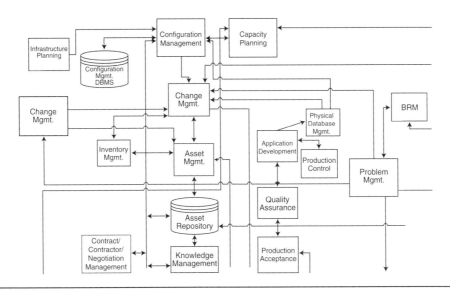

Figure 2.1 Process Representations—Database and Flowchart

Process Maturity Modeling

Deriving its inspiration from CMM (see Figure 1.1 in Chapter 1), Process Maturity Modeling (PMM) ranks key development indicators in stages 1 to 5. It assesses key performance indicators for each process, calculating overall process performance. The PMM rating scheme ranges from 1 for immature to 5 for mature, and it measures the overall performance of an organization's processes over time. The following multiple weighting factors calculate the overall PMM:

- Goals
- Platform automation
- Process performance
- Organizational impact

The PMM uses a traffic-light coloring scheme on all its spreadsheets, often called "dashboards," as shown in Figure 2.2.

Goals

Goals are critical to every organization because they provide direction for the organization's efforts and they set the desired results against

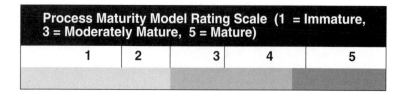

Figure 2.2 Process Maturity Modeling Rating Scale

which it judges individual or group performance. Organizations should use the goals for the operations excellence program to identify, prioritize, and fund process improvement efforts. Organizations should measure performance through a number of goal-oriented metrics.

Process improvement initiatives do little if process performance cannot be:

■ Tracked over time

■ Related back to the goals of the organization

Therefore, identification and tracking of metrics for each operational goal are critical to the organization's ability to pinpoint performance.

An organization should identify a total of three key metrics for each operational goal. For example, if one key operational goal is to improve customer satisfaction, appropriate metrics to capture that goal's performance might include "the number of help desk inquiries closed on the first call," that is, the first-call resolution rate. To identify performance over time, the PMM should include the following:

■ An ongoing metric goal value, such as to increase customer satisfaction by 0.5 percent annually

■ A historical performance with the metric

■ An end-goal value for the metric, such as a 93-percent rate for first-call resolution

■ A date by which the goal should be achieved

These values provide a baseline for metric performance.

Organizations should capture metrics via regular scheduled observation points. These metrics should capture three data elements:

■ The existing value of the metric

- The variance of the metric from the historic value
- The variance of the metric from the goal

Platform Automation

Automation is the linchpin of any service provider business model. An operations organization should formally track and manage the level of automation within each process. Understanding the level of automation often drives early investment decisions around operations excellence initiatives.

Many processes, such as workload monitoring, have long been automated in mainframe environments. But the introduction of client/server and Web-based technologies has resulted in the loss of automation within specific processes, such as performance monitoring. This lack of automation can be the primary impediment to providing an end-to-end management view of business applications.

The PMM rates performance of the automation tools for each operational process on each platform, such as mainframes, UNIX, Windows 2000/.NET server, and so on. Organizations should aggregate the results and calculate an overall automation level for each process. After being calculated using the 1-to-10 scale mentioned earlier, where 1=manual and 10=fully automated, the process automation level should be incorporated automatically into the overall process ratings.

Process Performance

Process performance is critical to operational excellence. The PMM identifies five variables that determine the organization's overall process performance:

- Definition (such as workflows and assumptions)
- Integration
- Skills or staffing
- Tools or automation
- Metrics

The PMM defines five levels of maturity in relation to each of the five process elements. Utilizing the maturity definitions, organizations should make a subjective rating of the maturity of each process. Results are weighted and an overall process performance score is calculated.

Organizational Impact

Although identifying process performance alone has value, organizations must measure the impact that other business-oriented variables have on its process performance, such as the following:

- The organization's culture
- The ability or willingness of the organization to change
- The process improvement priorities

Many organizations find that, for whatever reason, investments made to process improvement seldom yield substantial (and sustainable) returns. Similarly, some of the organization's business drivers will rapidly change the organization's processes, making short-term measurement difficult.

The priorities calculated as a result of the PMM exercises would enable the organization to focus efforts on those processes that can be best affected by additional investment in time and resources.

Process Maturity Modeling Characteristics

After the goals, process performance, automation, and organizational impact have been assessed by tracking them on a spreadsheet, a process maturity rating should be assigned to each process.

The following ratings, largely derived by META Group from the CMM, should be used to assess process maturity.

Level 1—Ad Hoc Random

Level 1 is the farthest away from being a best practice because no planning or structure is applied.

- The processes are not defined or documented in the process catalog.
- Process tasks are performed in an ad hoc manner with personal initiatives becoming the driving force. Processes have an implicit and informal character. Consequently, the operating assumptions are unknown and the experience and know-how is not leveraged.
- No relationship exists between service supply and demand, and the operation uses very little or no automation.
- Operational processes are not known; thus, they are not audited.
- Operational data is rarely collected, if at all.
- Lines of business (LOBs) hardly perceive any value.

Level 2—Repeatable

Level 2 includes a minimal amount of planning and documentation, which allows the process to be repeatable but does not allow for consistent execution.

■ The processes are partially documented in terms of workflows and relationships, but little or no agreement exists regarding execution. Staff awareness and commitment occurs on key operational processes.

■ The corrective actions to remedy service failures are inconsistent despite involvement of the same resources. In crisis situations, the processes typically are bypassed.

■ The focus is on operational control, for which automation tools are chosen for tactical reasons with a narrow focus.

■ Although known, the operational processes are not audited.

■ Operational data is regularly collected, primarily for reporting purposes, but is not controlled due to lack of standards.

■ LOBs perceive value in very vague terms; service levels are not established.

Level 3—Defined

Level 3 is a "better practice" because sufficient planning, documentation and discipline are used to make these repeatable processes that are executed consistently. It is not a best practice, however, because no provision is made for adaptation to changing business requirements.

■ Key operational processes are fully documented, monitored, and measured on the basis of targets that are defined in terms of first-generation SLA metrics, primarily focusing on performance, and in terms of standards that are predominantly self-chosen and internal. Process workflows, roles, and responsibilities are defined, and agreement on how processes should be performed is reached.

■ When service failures occur, or in crisis situations, the processes are always performed. Service failures are remedied through consistent, corrective actions, albeit in reactive mode, from staff having a "hands on" feeling of operational confidence.

■ An "internal fit" is pursued, with users shifting focus from operational control to service control. Automation is broadly scoped.

Innovation efforts are triggered when service levels are repeatedly exceeded.

■ Operational processes are audited occasionally to adjust service levels.

■ Extensive reports encompassing key metrics are produced, but modest feedback is sought.

■ LOBs perceive generic value. Service-level expectations are described in terms of technology metrics.

Level 4—Managed

Level 4 moves us closer to a best practice because processes are not only repeatable and consistent, but provision is made for adaptation based on feedback from LOBs. Level 4 is missing a way to optimize the process for maximum efficiency and effectiveness.

■ The processes are fully documented, monitored, and measured on the basis of targets that are defined in terms of second-generation SLA metrics, encompassing cost, performance, service quality, and customer satisfaction, and in terms of standards that are service-oriented, or fine-tuned to the external environment. Process inter-relationships and service cycles are defined.

■ Service failures and crises are reduced to a minimum, and processes are moderately integrated, expediting service production.

■ "Internal fit" is achieved, with users shifting focus from service production to service consumption and tuning service levels to address changing business needs and requirements. LOBs have an influence on service-level definitions. Automation is viewed as a key enabler, and innovation needs are identified even before service levels are exceeded.

■ Operational processes are periodically audited to refine SLAs, and customer feedback is sought proactively.

■ LOBs perceive extended value. Service-level expectations are described in terms of second-generation metrics.

Level 5—Optimized

Level 5 is a best practice. Processes are repeatable, consistent, adaptable, and optimized for maximum efficiency and effectiveness. The methods used to adapt and optimize the processes are based on sophisticated, customer-oriented metrics and tools.

- The processes are fully documented, monitored, and measured on the basis of targets that are defined in terms of service value agreements (SVA) metrics, which encompass cost, performance, service quality, customer satisfaction, business results, and impacts, and also in terms of standards that are customer-driven, or derived from the external environment. IT and business process relationships are determined.

- Corrective actions are embedded into the processes. Automation tools are chosen for strategic reasons. The ability to adapt to changing internal and external conditions is based on the fact that processes are well integrated and improvement is continually sought.

- "External fit" is pursued, by which users shift focus to balancing service supply and demand overtime, and LOBs determine the service levels.

- Operational processes are audited on an ongoing basis, as part of continuous improvement, to refine SVAs and to better understand the business results and impact.

- LOB value perceptions exceed expectations. Service-level expectations are described in terms of SVA metrics.

Extending Process Reach

Operational processes are a balance of manual and automated tasks. As processes become stable or "commoditized," they introduce opportunities for automation. Automation and integration trigger "stepwise" process improvements (see Figure 2.3). The level of automation is an early indicator showing organizations where they should focus investments. In fact, automation is the linchpin of every service provider's business model.

Some processes, such as job scheduling in the mainframe environment, have become commoditized. Such processes lend themselves to high degrees of automation and are supported heavily by a competitive set of automation tools. Generally, vendor offerings tend to appear only when components of the process have reached this commoditization level, such as when the process is executed over a common infrastructure.

Other processes are difficult to normalize to a common semantic structure and a reasonable set of repeatable tasks. Diverse infrastruc-

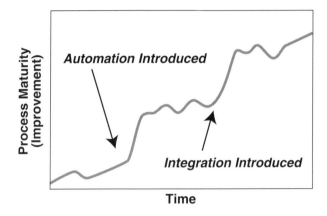

Figure 2.3 Typical Impact of Automation and Integration on Process Efficiency

ture, applications, or multiple constituencies' needs require complexity that moves these processes beyond the commodity level.

This chapter presented the concept of tasks and processes. It then discussed how to roll up tasks into processes. It also demonstrated how to inventory processes to develop a process catalog. As Chapter 3 explains, this catalog is a fundamental document in the pursuit of operational excellence. Finally, this chapter gave a glimpse of coming discussions of how processes can be refined, advanced, and improved. Chapter 3 examines how the process catalog is used to refine processes.

Chapter **3**

Gap Analysis and Process Refinement

Chapter 2 explained how to develop a process catalog that looks like the one in Chapter 7 with two notable differences: Your catalog will reflect your firm's operations, and it should be considerably shorter than the sample in the Chapter 7 because most sites only have a subset of the complete catalog. If you have not already done so, you should stop here and develop the process catalog for your IT operations. All subsequent discussion in this book presumes that you have completed this crucial step.

Gap Analysis

Gap analysis is a fundamental technique of best-practices implementation. It consists of finding gaps between the current state of operations, known as the baseline, and a hoped-for design known as the target. The target generally includes best practices, and the migration toward it is the raison d'être for the entire project. In many cases, the company designs the target at the start of the project, basing the decisions upon the needs the project seeks to address.

Gap analyses can use other targets depending on what the analyses seek to ascertain. For example, in this chapter, rather than entering into the formulation of such a project target, the gap analysis compares the process catalog designed by you in Chapter 2 with the process catalog presented in Chapter 7. The goal is to determine whether any tasks are missing from the processes in the baseline. This verification is important because managers who are unaware that a given process is missing an important task could engage in a fruitless attempt to improve the process. So, the first step in a good gap analysis is to ascertain what is missing. Later, gaps in quality between the baseline implementation and the target can be analyzed and addressed.

The next section performs a gap analysis to verify completeness for the process of change management, as an example. To follow the steps, you should examine the pages on the change management process in Chapter 7 and the corresponding pages in your process catalog.

Example of Gap Analysis: Change Management

Change management is the process of handling changes and requests for changes in an enterprise. Almost every enterprise with an IT organization performs change management. Very few firms will have a process catalog that does not include change management. Change management frequently represents a big headache for most IT organizations. Hence, application of best practices to change management is likely to be an important benefit for operations and for the company in general.

First, compare your definition of the description of change management in Chapter 7. Does your process handle the four stated activities of change management? If not, you must determine why not. Are the target purposes located in other processes? If so, you need to cull them from those documents and move them to the change management process. Are the target purposes not performed in your organization as part of change management? If your site does not perform all four activities as part of change management, you need to note and, more importantly, fix this gap. The change management process should handle, coordinate, and rationalize changes, and it should set policy. If change management policy is set by another process, improving change management will be nearly impossible, and any pursuit of best practices in change management will be condemned to failure.

The items in the "Tasks" section of any process entry in Chapter 7 are the tasks defined earlier for change management. These tasks are what this exercise focuses on:

■ Does your IT organization maintain an ongoing process of accepting requests, analyzing them, submitting them to management, and then processing according to feedback?

■ Does your IT organization have integrated processes for all aspects of change management?

■ Does your firm have a process to be sure that back-out provisions exist for all changes?

If these three questions do not meet affirmative answers, gaps between the baseline and the target have been identified. These gaps should be carefully documented. They become an important part of the process-improvement work in subsequent chapters.

Performing even this preliminary gap analysis on the processes inventoried in the baseline document produces immediate benefit. Done properly, this exercise could uncover dozens of gaps. Simply knowing what the gaps are contributes greatly to an appreciation of the need for quality enhancement.

Table 3.1 shows a sample form for recording gaps as they are found, although many other form designs are equally useful.

This form contains several fields that require further explanation.

■ Priority: This field will be filled in later when it is time to assign priorities to the tasks that need to be added.

■ Level of Automation: The level of automation, based on a scale from 1 to 10, with 10 being completely automated, helps establish

Table 3.1 A Sample Form for Recording Gaps Caused by Missing Tasks

Process:_____		Level of Automation (1–10)	Enablers (S=staff/skills, P=procedures, T=tools, A=all)				
Missing Tasks	Priority		PCs	UNIX	OS/390	Network	Other

the priority for addressing the gap. Manual tasks require more investment of time and money and so may be pushed back.

■ Enablers: These describe the resources necessary to close the gap. Some resources may depend on specific platforms; use the appropriate platform column for them. Initially, if you find it difficult to know what enablers are required, leave this area blank. Ultimately, before you decide which gaps to close, you must fill in the necessary enablers.

Not all gaps discovered in this process signify a problem. Some sites might have excellent processes in place but have constraints or unique situations that preclude the task list, as shown in the process catalog, from applying uniformly to them. IT organizations at such businesses likely will recognize processes where these divergences occur and will recognize that these "gaps" do not represent a problem.

Continuing with Gap Analysis

Performing gap analysis on all processes in the baseline generates a long list of gaps in the process. Acting on this list can take one of two forms:

■ You can choose to keep this list and proceed to the next steps of process refinement. This path eventually leads to the creation of centers of excellence (COEs). It is the "full treatment" provided by this book. This path is oriented toward companies that are completely committed to best-of-breed IT operations and are willing to make the considerable changes and investments necessary to reach this goal. Readers who are certain that this path is their choice can skip directly to "Process Refinement" later in this chapter.

■ The previous option is the main trunk of the book. Many organizations today, however, should consider the branch available to them at this juncture: using gap analysis as the principal mechanism of quality improvement and pursuit of best practices. This approach relies on deeper gap analysis and uses an alternative sequence of steps to act on the gaps, described in the following section, "Deeper Gap Analysis." Industry analyst firms project that fewer than 30 percent of IT sites perform gap analysis, while fewer than 10 percent pursue COEs. So choosing the path of strict gap analysis is likely to place your firm well ahead of all but the most-sophisticated IT organizations.

If you are uncertain which path to choose, the best course is to continue reading the book sequentially. Read about the gap analysis path as explained in the next few sections. Then continue with the progress toward process refinement and COEs. By the time you have finished the next two chapters, you will know which path is best for your site. The rest of this section, then, is directed toward readers curious about the second option, going no further than gap analysis.

Deeper Gap Analysis

After all processes in the baseline have undergone gap analysis, you examine the list of gaps to eliminate duplications and then prioritize them for remediation. This work generates a complete list of prioritized tasks. At that point, the person in charge of this project can determine how much time and money to spend, and hence which gaps to close. He knows that the list makes sense and the proposed sequence of steps leads directly to improved IT operations. If all gaps are closed, he has raised the base level of operations to the point where best practices can be considered. The work done so far has enabled your IT operations staff to perform the same tasks as benchmark industry practices at large firms.

To perform deeper gap analysis, you must fill out the form in Table 3.1 completely. Compare the skill sets required and the tools required for the process. Make sure that your firm has the right people doing the work with the right tools. Often the cause of a site not performing one of the tasks on the target list is a shortfall in personnel, skills, or tools such as software. Sometimes it's a combination of all three. The appropriate box should be checked under the category of enablers. These boxes become useful later, when consolidating the gaps. Patterns become especially obvious: Shortfalls in software or training, for example, become quantifiable and apparent, and they enable managers to pursue the remedies that are most effective for their site.

Finding the gaps in these areas is not a simple checklist exercise. Deciding what constitutes a gap can require careful analysis. Consider again the example of change management. The staffing suggests a change specialist and a change coordinator. Most sites have individuals in these roles. Business-to-IT liaisons exist at many sites as well. But what about the impact-assessment specialist? Employing this individual avoids the problem of making a change requested by Department X and inadvertently preventing Department Y from doing its work. Clearly, this is an important position whose responsibilities are all too frequently distributed among senior IT staffers. Best practices in change management cannot occur without this person. Typically, this specialist needs a very deep understanding of all the activities that make up the company's business. He has a sense of all computer users' needs, what files and systems they use, and what they do with the data. He also must have a comprehensive understanding of the IT systems: how the systems work together, where critical files are stored, how access is provided, and so forth. This allows him to recognize that a change to database K will affect Department L's ability to close sales for the quarter. Change management is an unusual process: It frequently is not integrated with other processes, but it has touch points with almost every business activity and IT process.

So, in this example, it is an error to view the company's staffing in change management without noting a gap if the impact-assessment specialist is not a dedicated position. The fact that this work is distributed among several IT staffers does not mean it's not a gap. Record it as such.

Likewise in software, if the company uses homegrown systems for change management, this situation needs expanded examination:

■ Is it homegrown for purely historical reasons?

■ Are vendor tools inadequate or too expensive?

■ What unique benefits does the homegrown solution deliver?

This situation should be marked as a gap except when the company has unique criteria that preclude the use of packaged software. In all other cases, homegrown solutions that duplicate packaged solutions and contribute to shortfalls in process quality need to be evaluated carefully. Companies, of course, do have cultural reasons for keeping old homegrown tools, but these considerations should not dissuade you from recording a gap where one exists.

Finally, the gap analysis should include *integration points*, which are the places where a given process touches or intersects with other processes. For example, management of the customer relationship and management of any contractor relationships often have few overlaps, hence few points of integration; but database management and disk-storage management likely will have many overlaps, and thus have numerous points. Integration points help you to prioritize tasks. If certain changes affect one area repeatedly, the changes can be sequenced to minimize disruption to that area. Likewise, integration points highlight places where changes can be consolidated for purposes of economy. For example, suppose a homegrown system is affected by numerous tasks that require remediation. This situation might suggest replacing the system. In so doing, the IT organization could be handed a list of criteria that the new system must meet in its future position in enhanced IT operations.

To this end, the deeper gap analysis should use a form that reflects the points of integration. Table 3.2 represents such a form. Again, many variations are possible. Choose a form that captures this information in a way that is most accessible and suitable to your needs.

A useful way to store these completed forms once is in a small database. A database also makes it easier to sort on priorities, search for common touch points, and the like.

Table 3.2 An Expanded Form for Gap Analysis

Process:_____		Level of Automation (1–10)	Enablers (S=staff/skills, P=procedures, T=tools, A=all)				
Missing Tasks	Priority		PCs	UNIX	OS/390	Network	Other
Points of Integration:	1. 2.		5. 6.				
Date of Analysis / /200_	3. 4.		7. 8.				

After the Analysis

After the gaps have been inventoried, IT departments must work to resolve them. This process consists of a series of steps:

- Categorize the gaps.
- Prioritize the gaps.
- Identify and develop gap-filling scenarios.
- Fill the selected gaps.

An orderly procession of remedial work flows from this sequence of steps. And as the work progresses, quality improves throughout IT operations to the point where best practices can be considered, if not undertaken.

Categorizing the Gaps

Gaps should be categorized according to the nature of the originating gap. Categories that find common use in this regard include:

- *Structural gaps* point to problems in the structure of IT operations. Generally, these gaps include the wrong tools or missing tools.
- *Functional gaps* point to necessary functions that are not being performed. In this gap analysis, functional gaps are likely to be numerous.
- *Cultural gaps* are the gaps in skills, competence, and structure of the current IT operations and the skill, competence, and structure needed to support the gap resolution of the structural and functional gaps. Cultural gaps take a great deal of time and continuous reinforcement to maintain after they are changed. As a result, resolution of cultural gaps should be examined with particular care. Closing cultural gaps is likely to close other gaps, either completely or in part.
- *Procedural gaps* point to holes in operational procedures. They can be missing procedures, or they can be procedures missing an important step. Generally, these are among the easiest gaps to resolve.

The boxes marked "Enablers" in Tables 3.1 and 3.2 help identify a category into which various gaps fit.

Prioritizing the Gaps

After the gaps have been categorized, they must be prioritized. Prioritization should be based on a filter of sorts. This filter pushes the highest priorities to the top of the list. Designing the filter is a challenge unto itself. Important considerations include the following:

■ Urgency

■ Importance

■ Scope

■ Cost

■ Duration

■ Ease of implementation

■ Cultural factors

Urgency and importance are obviously key criteria and are self-explanatory, but the two are not synonymous. Urgent matters often acquire the patina of importance, especially in the domain of operations. Experienced managers generally can distinguish tactical urgency from strategic importance, and they can provide leadership in the application of this filter to the list of gaps.

The scope of a gap is very important to consider. As mentioned in the previous section on categorizing gaps, closing gaps of large scope often closes secondary gaps and exposes new ones. When given the choice, select the gaps of large scope before other gaps.

Cost is an inherent prioritizing factor. If a large, important gap requires substantial funding, you might need to re-prioritize other gaps on the basis of cost.

Duration and ease of implementation are self-explanatory. However, an important consideration in prioritizing is that quick, easy changes—which occur almost invariably in procedural gaps—can lead to immediate visible improvements in operations. Priority lists should include gaps of this kind to provide encouragement and the perception of a quick payoff for the quality-improvement efforts. The choice of a few of these tasks is primarily psychological. If the changes are being made in a culture that is not wholly supportive, inclusion of these tasks is mandatory.

Gap-Filling Scenarios

After a prioritized gap list is drawn up and agreed to, the IT organization should develop scenarios for closing the gaps. This step requires thoughtful managers with experience in operations. Depending on the scope of the changes, scenarios mean very substantial changes to the way things are done. When large-scale changes are considered, three possible processes come into play. They are described in Table 3.3.

Changes on this scale suggest doing more than closing the existing gaps. They favor implementing best practices at the same time. Hence for the identified processes, a custom gap analysis between the baseline and the best practices, as found in Chapter 7, is required. This analysis leads to additional steps in the projects but avoids decisions that encumber a later move to best practices.

When developing scenarios, several traps must be sidestepped, as they are sure to appear:

■ Avoid groupthink. Many IT initiatives have been killed by "groupthink" as team members share common but unspoken ideas about what is happening and divergent opinions are consciously or

Table 3.3 Processes for Large-scale Gap-filling Scenarios

Process	Description	Benefits	Risks
Forward Engineering	Starting from a clean slate, the gap-filling exercise is done, looking for new best-practice solutions and systems.	No legacy limitations. Aligned with the established business vision.	Requires vision and detail. Is costly and has a higher risk. Established rules no longer apply.
Re-engineering in place	The current environment is decomposed and a tailored solution to support the identified gap(s) is developed.	Preserves the established rules. Lowers risk and cost of implementation and maintenance.	Straddles both the legacy and future visions. Requires planned systems rework. May still carry over old ways of doing things.
Reverse re-engineering	The current environment is decomposed and existing functions are rebuilt to support the identified gaps.	Preserves the established rules. Exploits new technology using existing and understood rules and functions.	The cost and time to find the right solution are greater than that for re-engineering in place.

unconsciously discouraged. Scenario planning forces the individual team members to consider uncomfortable possibilities. Each member brings something different to the exercise, depending on individual responsibilities, experiences, beliefs, and assumptions. Inconsistent ideas about the gap, the supported vision, and its objectives are uncovered during the scenario-planning exercise.

- Anticipate denial. Even experienced project managers can fail to see problems until they become fires. Preparing for the inevitable problems will sensitize team members to seeing problems as they start to happen and before they get out of control.

- Resist accelerating action. When glitches inevitably occur, pressure to respond mounts, multiplying opportunities for bad decisions, quick fixes, and inelegant workarounds. Scenario planning enables the emotional reactions that lead to bad decision-making to be played out before a crisis happens.

Many scenarios need not change on the scale discussed here. However, they still need to be developed with the same caution. Many times, the scenarios will be smaller, self-contained, and well understood. This smaller scale could lead to a false sense of security, especially if an unanticipated glitch occurs during implementation. Review traps 2 and 3 from the preceding list with care when developing the scenarios.

After the scenarios are developed, they should be scheduled and implemented using standard project-management tools and techniques.

What Then?

As mentioned previously in this chapter, many firms do not go beyond gap analysis and resolution in their efforts to improve operations. Companies that choose this path, though, must be vigilant about the formation of new gaps. Performing regularly scheduled gap analysis represents the most effective way of remaining vigilant. Many firms commit to a six-month schedule of gap analysis. In this scenario, the process catalog is updated and compared to the established standard to determine whether new gaps have occurred.

After a site has stabilized and all the important gaps have been closed, the group can pursue best practices. To do this, the baseline document should be compared against the best practices listed for processes in Chapter 7. This comparison generates many new gaps for even well-run IT organizations. These gaps should be handled by the procedures discussed in the preceding sections. In addition, pursuing best practices requires the implementation of metrics. Chapter 5 of this book shows how to incorporate and use metrics in the quest for best practices. This chapter should be read and understood by departments choosing to follow this path.

The remainder of this chapter discusses process refinement. It picks up from the earlier point where the gap analysis was completed, but no follow-up steps to the analysis had been undertaken.

Process Refinement

True end-to-end management of operations requires the elimination of islands of data, or autonomous processes also known as "stovepipes," and a strong focus on maximizing efficiency with a directed effort at long-term unit cost reduction. The goal is to unify the staff, technology, and processes into a seamless organization. The creation of processes and centers of excellence (COEs) is a key stage in this operations excellence effort.

Processes generally are of minimal interest to end users, who typically want to access the corporate network, Web, or other IT service without thinking about the infrastructure and services that lie beneath. The services define an organization's operations to end users within the company—who are in essence the IT department's customers. The services are what these customers "buy" from the IT organization.

Because of this relationship of customer and provider, processes and COEs are important parts of attaining excellence in operations. End-to-end, repeatable processes instantiate best practices throughout the operations organization. Related processes coalesce into COEs. The focus on refining process and COEs supports improvement in two areas:

- Operations efficiency. Process-centric organizations work continually on doing things "better, faster, cheaper." When measured, these improvements may be only in the single digits on an annualized percentage basis. Over the course of several years, however, the improvements become significant, and they separate best-in-class companies from the also-rans.

- Definition, development, pricing, and market services offered to users within the organization. Processes and COEs take much of the guesswork out of creating services, and this increased certainty can be reflected back to the end-user constituencies who are your customers. And customers generally prefer an integrated, holistic approach.

The COE model demands that operations groups become organizationally and functionally process-centric to deliver near-seamless service for new and legacy applications and integration between the two. Organizations not focused on process performance and improvement cannot graduate to COEs.

Creating both processes and COEs requires investment, both financial and emotional. Financially speaking, the operations group involved in process refinement and COE development must devote resources to the areas where they will do the most good. Also, before getting started an organization must decide whether its operations team has the human resources and energy needed to reshape itself and the organization.

Ownership of tasks and, later, processes is an important issue. In smaller organizations, tasks tend to be owned by individuals. In larger groups, task ownership is more like a partnership arrangement, and these partners may be within different parts of the organization.

Process refinement can be undertaken as a prelude to migration to COEs. As such, it requires consideration of the factors described in the rest of this chapter.

Process Evolution

Even with proper attention to process metrics and continuous process feedback, only incremental improvements occur without the infusion of an automating technology or process integration. For example, you might drive costs out of the process execution. Process automation can dramatically increase the IT operation's maturity and should be measurable on process efficiency and effectiveness scales. Other major maturity steps occur at the points of basic (and complex) cross-process integration.

The advent of change within the environment under the auspices of a particular process is one of the largest contributors to process dysfunction. *Less frequently, it can act as a catalyst to automation.* In general, though, change represents a major inhibitor to process improvement and maturity, as shown in Figure 3.1.

In addition, operational processes stagnate because of inattention, insufficient resources, and limited formal process definitions. The latter is a problem in new process areas such as enterprise resource planning, customer relationship management, and e-Business.

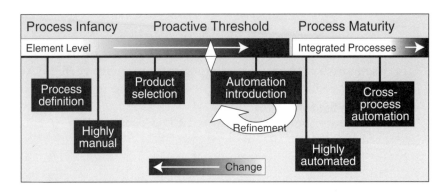

Figure 3.1 Process Evolution (or Revolution)

Process relevance can change over time. Operation organizations overemphasizing process metrics, such as inputs/outputs, direct/allocated costs, staffing levels, stability, and so on, typically focus on meeting performance targets and output quotas. Meanwhile, they overlook process relevance and its role in infusing operational excellence. People in such organizations rarely question how processes are carried out, assuming that business or technology changes will not affect value-generating processes.

Prolonged process stability can result in a staff obsession with established policies—even when the reasons for doing so are no longer valid. The results are service inflexibility and missed opportunities to improve performance by exploiting change within relevant processes. Organizations should address the impact of changing business conditions on process relevance. Processes can be refined reactively, in response to demands from the business, or proactively, to create a source of value within the operations organization.

Operations groups must establish a two-part framework for process improvement. First, they must identify current and future best practices for each operational process within their catalog. Staff resources should focus on improving baseline capabilities and use metrics to define excellence and investment prioritization. Second, the process catalog enables rapid response teams to assess new workloads and to identify skill gaps while insulating core teams from change.

Technology enables the implementation of process methodologies, but it does not deploy the methodology "out of the box." In fact, most technology simply deploys process methodology, and organizations should concentrate selection criteria based on a given technology's ability to deploy flexible processes, rather than on certification requirements.

Change efforts scoped around every process within the organization simply are not feasible. Organizations should pare down lengthy lists to processes that matter most, focusing on two key process attributes: relevance and value contribution.

Process Innovation

Operational process innovation enables businesses to better position IT investments along with other expenditures and improve cross-functional capacity. Groups should focus process innovation efforts primarily on high-relevance, asset-producing processes, adopting an inclusive approach and taking into account that process relevance changes over time.

The challenges for most IT groups are assessing whether specific processes have a positive or negative impact on performance and identifying the most relevant processes to infuse operational excellence. Some attempt diverse innovation approaches in the hope of getting one right, directing human and financial capital on disruptive and sometimes disappointing initiatives. Others pursue quick fixes and short-term cost efficiencies, engaging themselves in simplifications—processes that are easy to analyze and measure—that are superficially attractive (and may not be most relevant). Thus, they risk investing in the wrong processes or employing inappropriate approaches that may lead to the process paradox: measurable process improvement accompanied by measurable performance decline. Indeed, failure to improve operational performance often results from "getting the process right," instead of "getting the right process right."

A process-oriented or product-focused operations organization must develop one or more approaches to fostering innovation and extracting additional efficiency, and thus value, from its processes. Organizations that shy away from the issue of process reform or fail to innovate will remain in demand but will be considered less valued components.

Although many ways to foster innovation exist, no generally accepted method is inherently superior to another, and no single approach addresses every operational process problem. Most efforts at process improvement spring from an internal perspective; they are a reaction to issues internal to the operations organization instead of a proactive effort or a response to external forces.

Using a particular innovation technique often creates opportunities to use others, sometimes even concurrently. Applying this approach, however, can be difficult to coordinate and plan. IT groups should start with a single approach and a small set of processes to gain experience—and demonstrate success—before treating critical processes or more complex settings.

Before assessing the extent of incurred changes and the likelihood of success in process adjustments, improvements, or breakthroughs, IT groups should recognize the service failure points and processes that cause them.

Ad Hoc Adjustments

These adjustments include abandoning, front-ending, automating, standardizing, outsourcing, or co-sourcing processes. By tidying up a process without incurring significant costs, unacceptable risks, or organizational changes, organizations can achieve short-term benefits without analyzing the process detail or rethinking its purpose. Adjustments rarely create value directly, but they can preserve value and provide options for delivery. Organizations should apply this approach to low-priority processes.

Continuous Improvement

Continuous improvement is the hard work of innovation. Here, it encompasses streamlining, integrating, and centralizing processes. Such an evolutionary approach can generate long-lasting value, but it requires organizations to undergo thorough process analysis and invest significantly to sustain improvements. Underestimating these investments or anticipating unrealistic, short-term payoffs often can undermine the likelihood of success.

Major Breakthroughs

This area covers restructuring, importing, exporting, and designing new processes. It involves radical approaches, which entail higher risk and involve more fundamental changes than other types of innovation. Such an approach will be reflected in the way operations organizations are viewed by their customers. However, major breakthroughs yield substantial payoffs and sustained operational excellence, taking operational process reform beyond ad hoc adjustments and continuous improvements.

Innovation induces diverse levels of change, each with unique, potential risks and returns. IT groups should undertake innovation efforts with a level of change that matches the capabilities and culture of their organization. With a continuous improvement approach, for example, the risk of failure is relatively low. Therefore, those efforts should involve a simple, standardized approach to continuous improvement that is applied to many processes throughout the organization. An effort to pursue major breakthroughs demands the opposite approach, whereby organizations apply different innovation techniques to a limited number of processes.

Regardless of whether an organization feels comfortable with incremental improvements (and predictable changes) or whether it needs to adopt more radical approaches, management commitment will be a critical success factor. In addition to influencing the type of processes targeted for reform and the innovation techniques applied to them, the degree of management commitment determines the likelihood of success.

Process Integration

End-to-end-processes ensure consistent service delivery and improve customer satisfaction. Establishing such processes requires close attention to the linkages among these processes and the handover points within the organizational structure. A fragmented approach can weaken end-to-end service focus, duplicate process tasks, and lengthen the process development life cycle.

Even when an organization has operational processes that have worked long and well within data centers, creating support for integrated processes can be problematic. Typically, the problems with communication or coordination resulting from loosely integrated processes in data centers are resolved because groups work in proximity. However, employing such process silos in distributed computing is ineffective because the spaces between processes increase dramatically, incurring significant coordination costs and making it difficult to identify accountability.

Increased outsourcing means that the operations organization may operate across diverse boundaries—exacerbating the coordination of different processes and management of multiple relationships, hindering organizational development, and delaying change programs. In fact, business process changes often precede those of IT operations, and as customers assimilate new applications, service gaps and program delays become more noticeable. Additionally, operations organizations are perceived as unresponsive—especially in the absence of bridging mechanisms such as governance, relationship management, and steering committees that oversee business and technology changes.

Operational process innovation enables businesses to better position IT and other investments and to improve cross-functional capabilities. To create end-to-end service transactions and control over delivery during process innovation efforts, IT groups must establish a matrix-based organization where vertical management structures that are focused on staff coexist with means of lateral coordination that are focused on processes.

Specific capabilities and skills built on operational processes ultimately support COE models. These models are less hierarchical; are more service-oriented and customer-focused; and involve new reporting paths, performance measurements, roles, and responsibilities.

Horizontal operations processes, combined with vertical management hierarchies, along technology domains, functions, geographies, and so on, often give rise to voids and overlaps. Processes drive operations staff in one direction, while management systems pull them in another. This can cause service failures and undermine operational performance.

Changing service needs exacerbate this issue, compelling operations organizations to reassess the "structure follows strategy" paradigm and continually reconcile organizational and process structures. Process integration efforts should shift focus from the structure of processes to their underlying purpose. In the COE model, these efforts end at well-defined points of service to customers.

Adopting such a model may help an organization avoid perpetuating debates regarding the appropriateness of organizational structures and focus on measuring/improving operational processes in terms of business benefits, costs, and service quality/cycles. Such an approach also provides operations staff with an unambiguous view of how their work fits into IT operations.

Process integration requires process owners to lead innovation efforts and coordinate process requirements with line management. The role of the owners cuts across organizational functions, creating a virtual matrix where process owners are accountable for the quality of their work in support of the processes.

The role of the process owner encompasses oversight and guidance. However, separating process from people management induces a split of authority, making cooperation between process owners and line managers obligatory, a situation that many operations organizations find difficult.

Process owners design processes, set performance targets, and ensure process continuity or control across multiple functions by establishing mechanisms to recover from service failures when processes break down. They are responsible for ongoing process improvement efforts and oversee cross-functional process effectiveness.

The choice of process owners is paramount in communicating commitment to process innovation efforts and ensuring that the company takes them seriously. Along with strong skills in teamwork, facilitation, communication, and project management, owners must be cognizant of technologies and activities involved in making the processes work. To strive for continuous process improvement and ensure that organizational strictures do not reassert themselves, best-in-class organizations view process ownership as a permanent position.

Superimposing processes on vertical organizations requires new working relationships across lateral organizational boundaries. These relationships should emphasize service over turf or hierarchies and end-to-end processes rather than narrow tasks.

Such changes require a major cultural adjustment and significant management commitment. Documenting roles, responsibilities, decision rights, staffing or budgeting policies, and change management actions in a road map for management teamwork helps resolve disagreements that might arise.

The road map also should facilitate collaboration among process owners that resolves resource conflicts by reviewing or coordinating such items as operational plans, resource schedules, budgets, service levels, and performance measures.

Taking the process focus to this level of organization and integration does not happen overnight. However, many IT groups are eager to move directly to the end game, bypassing their opening moves. To avoid getting drawn into sea-of-change programs triggered by process innovation efforts, organizations should allocate higher priority to those that promise substantial payoffs. Ultimately, well-refined, integrated processes, when aligned with the organization, permit centers of excellence.

Centers of Excellence

Centers of excellence (COEs) represent a unique organizational entity that contains a mix of task, process, and "brain trust" personnel. COEs represent a higher level of synergy when compared to traditional organizational structures.

This chapter defines five COEs. Chapter 4 goes into detail regarding the creation of these and other COEs.

Command Center COE. This service ensures maximum availability and throughput. Tasks include monitoring of systems, peripherals, and networks; all processes affecting availability are included here as well. This group would take the lead in automation efforts, although each of the other COEs would require specialized automation. Roles within the command center are the most esoteric of any within operations groups, making automation the primary success factor.

Service Center COE. This provides a single point of interaction for IT operations and includes help desk, production control, business account managers, and security administration. Building a service matrix, metrics, SLA support, and customer advocacy are the major challenges for this unit.

Data/Media Center COE. This COE includes all tasks related to managing data, data storage, data output, disaster recovery, and databases. Minimizing risk and reacting to new business initiatives are the major challenges for this group.

Asset Management COE. This service centralizes efforts around budgeting, charge-back, and inventory, as well as configuration, license, and hardware/software portfolio management. New tools and processes that address S/390 and non-S/390 resources are important vehicles for cutting costs and unifying decision making regarding enterprise assets. This activity is where the justification of operations value should be produced.

Application Management COE. The role of this group is to ensure that applications are managed appropriately and tied to both service-level and operational documentation processes. This is the second area where rapid response teams will be crucial—bringing the interests of operations into the development/deployment of new applications earlier. Impact assessments will be a core competency of this group.

Moving from Processes to COEs

Creating COEs represents both a workflow paradigm and an organizational construct. IT groups should take this organizational step slowly and cautiously, after several cross-functional teams have spent time working together to define and refine the tasks, processes, and automation that represent the full scope of responsibility associated with a given COE.

However, because only a small percentage of companies have attained this goal and established COEs, IT groups must understand the "look and feel" of a COE organization. The two unique aspects of the COE organization are the COE "brain trust" and the rapid-response team (RRT). These two groups, by definition, comprise the most powerful and knowledgeable staff. The brain trust focuses on process/COE improvement. The RRT covers assimilation of new workloads.

These groups require both operational and nontechnical skill sets. COEs blur the lines between traditional technical support groups and the day-to-day operations staff. COEs will expand to become more self-sufficient with regard to both the operational and technical roles inherent in each COE.

Within a given COE, 10 to 20 percent of staff represents the general COE management, analyzing and improving the many processes contained within the COE and, perhaps more importantly, managing the seams between one COE and another.

Although each COE is meant to be relatively autonomous by virtue of including closely related tasks and processes within its purview, the brain trust also represents the glue that ties multiple COEs together to represent a cohesive delivery strategy. The brain trust also makes decisions about how the group operates, devises new processes and procedures to increase efficiency and effectiveness, and ultimately defines the rules (that is, standards) by which customers must play to "earn" full support and service-level commitments from operations groups. The staff within this subgroup must have a clear understanding of the big picture and be capable of balancing customer needs with the appropriate set of prerequisites to ensure that operations groups can provide the desired support.

The RRT must play a distinctly different role from the brain trust, but it often contains some of the same staff, along with participants from the task and COE work teams.

The key role of the RRT is insulating core work teams from new workloads, domains, and other change agents. This role ensures that the COE can consistently deliver excellence with the appropriate amount of change introduced gradually (or as appropriate) from the RRT and brain trust groups. The RRT, therefore, cannot become a separate entity.

Leverage, end-to-end responsibility, and long-term unit cost reduction are the drivers for a COE, and in most cases, the RRT can bring back the information about new operational challenges to the brain trust, which would decide how and when to introduce the changes necessary for the new support.

Career development within a COE is greatly enriched. Although some staff members prefer to work at the task level and do not wish to move up within the COE, the career ladder is generally from the task level to the process level, moving to different areas within the process level, and then up to the COE brain trust. Participation in the RRT is also a career step, as its members deal more closely with clients and client issues and are more exposed within the organization due to the visibility of such projects.

The size of COE groups can range from three to four people in smaller companies to as many as 25 to 30 in very large companies. The principles are the same, however, given that COEs tend to leverage staff better and provide opportunities for cross training and career advancement at a much higher level than most current organizations, which are structured around stovepipe, plan/build/run, or projects.

COEs represent a higher level of synergy when compared with traditional organizational structures. Although COEs take three to four years to fully mature, organizational structures based on them should be implemented gradually, with careful attention paid to the individual orientation of each staff member.

Chapter 4

COEs—Building on the Process Foundation

COE-based IT organizations typically build delivery capability around services and products and promote a client-centric culture. They do so by creating innovative IT solutions to gain a competitive business advantage. Enterprises can foster COEs in several areas within the typical IT organization, such as assets, applications, command center, customer advocacy, data and media, engineering, outsourcing, and security. Most of these COEs will be discussed later in this chapter.

COE models appeal to IT organizations that intend to provide total IT solutions to business problems. IT support structures, such as repair and service-desk functions, also can benefit from COE best practices by helping to shape them into services that exceed client expectations at a competitive price.

However, creating COE organizations by merely restructuring IT functions around productized service portfolios, changing reporting lines, and evolving help desk functions to a customer call center will not make a significant difference, either to IT groups' performance or to business value. COE organizations must be established on a sound process foundation to deliver sustained service levels, have an intimate understanding of business needs, realize a fundamental IT cultural change, and cope with the fast proliferation of new technologies into the enterprise.

Most traditional IT organizations strive to increase business and IT synergies by promising technology applications that improve operational efficiencies. This approach typically results in limited cost containment or service improvements. Implementing COE services—such as desktop services, application subscriptions, or other such projects—without improving business performance, quality, status, prestige, and profit conflicts with the overall COE rationale.

Often, IT organizations create "artificial" COEs. These COEs involve a haphazard grouping of people and processes and may lack the enterprise wide focus of the true COE. In these artificial COEs, no previous benchmarks of performance exist. As a result, comparison to accepted levels of service or performance in the market at large is often difficult.

Failure to deliver true COEs success can result in a poor image for the IT organization, key IT personnel leaving the group, and even adverse affects on the core business.

COE Development

The first objective of COE development is to identify where grouping processes and improving process integration will optimize service and reduce cost.

Operations Optimization

Chapter 2 offered an approach for defining and refining tasks and processes that exist within your organization. Tasks and processes are the building blocks of the COE effort.

Prior to undertaking COE development, an enterprise must ensure that the operational house is in order, so to speak. Operations groups have become facilitators, in a sense. They ensure operations run not only efficiently, but also effectively—meeting the needs and expectations of both internal and external users. In such an environment, the service levels of the operations organization may be compared more frequently with those of experienced (and aggressive) providers of outsourced services. This compounds the necessity for the operations organization to function as an IT business, with an operations plan that includes well-defined product/service catalogs, user-understood pricing structures, and attention to service levels.

In addition, operations groups must tell the LOBs what they do and how well they do it. Therefore, for operations organizations to be successful, evidence of performance must be articulated to the business in terms it understands. The following are some key components that will assist operational organizations in realizing an operations plan:

- Identify the organization's goals.
- Identify metrics to track goal performance.
- Identify/define key operational processes (workflow, information flow, responsibilities).
- Integrate processes to reflect synergy.
- Quantify benefit back to the organization.
- Create centers of excellence around beneficial process groupings.

Identify the Organization's Goals

The identification of business goals and process definitions will be the first step on the way to the creation of an operations plan. This plan enables operations groups to better align resources with business requirements. A clearer understanding of the business value of such investments will drive improved investment decisions.

Although IT/business alignment has been discussed since the late 1980s, few within the IT organization can articulate business goals. As a result, products and services that are intended to be LOB-oriented often do not meet client satisfaction levels because of misaligned business/IT goals.

Identify Metrics to Track Goal Performance

One way for operations organizations to surmount this problem is by having the business units identify up to 10 business goals, such as processing a specific number of invoices per day. Identification of business goals will enable the operations group to better allocate resources and meet service levels, especially for newer technologies (for example, online ordering). The operations group then should identify three IT metrics for each business goal, reflecting the group's ability to meet those goals.

Identify/Define Key Operational Processes

Nearly 75 percent of operations groups are in the process of defining or refining their existing process sets. Because process performance is the core deliverable of operations groups, the creation of a process catalog is critical to successful delivery. The cataloging of processes goes beyond traditional workflows to include the identification of cross-process integration points, the recognition of automation tools, and accountability. Although organizations may have thousands of tasks that can be rolled up into hundreds of processes, operations groups should focus on the 30 to 40 processes that are critical to the group's performance and on the processes on which the operations group can best focus.

Integrate Processes to Reflect Synergy

Cross-process integration is another critical element in the maturity of operations groups and the evolution to COEs. COEs require cross-platform, end-to-end management of their related processes. Although many organizations understand the need to identify process-to-process hand-offs, such as change management and configuration management, most have not mapped the cross-process integration points, and even fewer have mapped the process-information flows—that is, the flows of information to and from particular processes, which are critical to process performance but do not readily appear on traditional process workflows.

Quantify Benefit Back to the Organization

In addition to the identification of goals and processes, the operations organization must allocate resources effectively while maintaining the traditional efficiency role within operations and adhering to task/process milestone expectations, assignment of responsibilities, and work prioritization. The operations organization must expand its traditional role, taking on a more strategic orientation focused on meeting deliverable expectations and time frames, as well as ensuring that resources are used most effectively. This requires proficiency in the articulation of service, resource planning, and attention to LOB service delivery. In addition, the operations organization must deliver evidence of performance to executive teams, making operations plan reporting (specifically the achievement of milestones and timing) a critical component.

With this combination of process organization and business goals in hand, the operations organization then should be able to do the following:

■ Map business drivers and the effects of technology changes, such as mergers, infrastructure consolidation, and new applications, on operational delivery processes as well as the resulting impact on existing operational groups.

- Map the effect of technology changes on the linkages between different operational groups.

- Manage the transition from existing operational groups to COEs prior to (or in conjunction with) implementing new technology.

Deliverables from this operations optimization effort should include:

- Identification of strengths/weaknesses within the IT organization.

- Prioritized to-do list for building COEs (see Table 4.1).

- Evaluation of what is and is not important to business customers.

- Tie-in to IT strategy.

In designing COEs, asking the following questions can help identify obstacles before you get to them:

- Do we understand how our operational processes relate to each other?

Table 4.1 List of Priorities for COE Design

Business Drivers	Application	Infrastructure	COE	Linkages
Improving ROI (New CIO) (Outstanding threat)	Application consolidation	Steady change	Asset Customer advocacy	Skills issue
Mergers/ acquisitions Organic growth	Selective deployment	Rapid change	Command Application Change management Data and media	Perceived position of new organization
New Web business model	Rapid deployment	Rapid change	Security Application	New skills needed
Outsourcing/ service provider	Steady change	Rapid change	Command Application Change management Data and media	Job losses and retraining
IT consolidation	Application consolidation	Infrastructure consolidation	Change management Customer advocacy	

- Could we improve delivery by moving processes into logical groupings?

- Are our existing process groupings, such as the command center, limited by organizational structure?

- Have we stovepiped our processes by platform type?

- From a delivery standpoint, are our operations world class?

- Do we practice "end-to-end" management?

- Are we using automation across processes effectively?

- Do we have metrics in place that track effectiveness within process groupings (centers of excellence)?

From Process to COE

At the COE level, processes tend to take on many of the characteristics of tasks when it comes to their place in the macro-level services that business areas recognize and expect in operations. However, if each process were performed in a vacuum, the economic benefits of managing and acquiring each of the associated resources would be lost. If there were no Data–and–Media COE, for example, but instead a separate focus on tape, DASD, database, and other components, the optimal selection of media and the use of the storage hierarchy to provide "just in time" service or "just enough" of the right resource would be impossible.

As most organizations evolve, they tend to move slowly but steadily to this sort of shared services model with focused skills centers. This reflects the organic nature of maturing organizations as they encounter skill commoditization and requirements for new services. The challenge is to establish the proper structure and framework to drive these centers to become COEs.

Without well-defined methods for creating, managing, and even exploiting centers, loosely confederated skills centers very rarely have the needed internal energy to move to the next plateau. In fact, most skills centers (for example, command and control) never mature to COEs, because important ingredients such as organization discipline, scope, and continuous improvement are not part of the organic infrastructure.

While offering more flexibility, COEs need both strong external and internal management initiatives for success. COEs do not necessarily work well together by default, and the external COE framework must have well-defined cross-center semantics. For example, COEs generally have business agreements for services with other COEs, just for this reason. In the same vein, COEs rarely solve staffing issues and more often create them. In most cases, for example, COEs still need task-like technical help, so organizations have, in many instances, two HR problems, not one. Consequently, the applied external framework must have well-defined recruitment and training objectives.

Another difficult challenge is business alignment. With empowered COE groups, the IT organization runs the risk that COE focus points may change, and a service considered critical by one may not have the same importance for another. This requires well-defined product life cycles. In addition, COEs currently considered critical might not have the same importance in the future, so sunset skills must be part of the organization. Another challenge is skill depth. Teaming can affect depth, and external COE governance must include review of skills and sourcing/recruitment alternatives.

Task/Process/COE Trade-offs

Although most organizations are aware that inherent organic organization changes lead to more general organization structures, the challenge is in the journey: the steps, methods, and environment needed to develop new operations generalists. These changes will inalterably modify the traditional depth-and-breadth skills mix.

The challenges faced by most task-based organizations as they migrate from a task-based approach to COEs change within the migration (see Figure 4.1). Most organizations have an ample supply of well-trained technicians who have focused expertise for providing support for traditional problems. All too often, these skill sets center around IT maintenance instead of on new challenges. Task-based groups are heavily weighted to the left of the diagram, which represents maintenance mode, and they are light on high-end integration and new technology skills. In fact, task-centric operations organizations, more often than not, go to the outside for help in these areas but very rarely learn new skills because the social system does not reward them.

However, operations organizations that have started the organization skills metamorphosis often are caught in the middle, needing help at both ends of the skills spectrum. Most are missing some high-end integration skills plus technology skills still needed for ongoing legacy survival. For this mid-journey position, operations groups must have access to both types of skills, and this puts more pressure on sourcing skills, including selective outsourcing. Considering that the transition from a

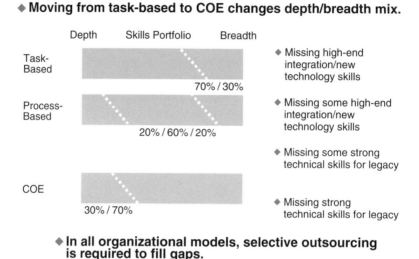

Figure 4.1 Task/COE Trade-offs

task-based approach to COE can easily last three to five years for large shops, sourcing skills should be a standard part of the infrastructure. This requires strong business support.

For organizations that have succeeded in implementing COEs, the sourcing challenge still exists. Like the previous two stages of the task-to-COE evolution, COE structures need strong sourcing skills at the bottom of the skills ladder. In addition, with slow migration from a task-based approach to COE more typical than not, ongoing skills gap analysis must remain an integral part of the infrastructure landscape.

For many operations organizations, a skills gap analysis is a singular event driven by a well-defined organization change. However, for operations organizations moving across the spectrum of organization alternatives, skills gap analysis must be an integral part of the restructuring plan and must be continually in play. For example, although strong specific OS/390 task-based skills may be in place—such as systems performance and changes to process—COE environments, which require more general cross-platform skills, will necessitate different levels and skills sets that complement changing internal skills. Consequently, skills gap sessions must be an integral part of the organization's journey and must actively drive sourcing decisions rather than simply being a quarterly exercise.

The COE Template

The COE template highlights the elements needed for a complete description of a COE. Examples of these templates as applied to many of the most common COEs appear in the COE catalog in Chapter 8.

COE Mission

Area of Expertise performs a discrete function or service that is owned by operations and can be delivered with excellence in execution. This excellence can be determined either by skill set possessed or by process refinement.

Binding Theme inherently sets the boundary, scope, and "governance" model for the function/service and delivery organization.

Value Proposition exhibits a credible, external value perception.

Processes covers the processes included in the COE, as well as related processes within the organization that must be addressed.

Skills refers to overall staff requirements, along with particular specialized job titles required.

Automation refers to available applications or solutions that automate either tasks or the entire process.

Best Practices are current and future techniques or activities utilized by leaders within this process.

Metrics are generally accepted or specialized measurements that help define the results of the process, both internally (process efficiency) and externally (process effectiveness). Also, they include specific measurements regarding the quantity and quality of changes made to the process.

Futures are changes to be made or discussed. How will changes in technology, vendors, service providers, business climate, and so forth affect the process?

The COE template varies from the process template outlined in Chapter 3 in several ways, but the key factor is the inclusion of the COE mission, which represents what customers will think about when evaluating operational services.

A Process Foundation

Technology-based organizations cannot succeed in transitioning to COE structures without building a solid process base. Operations organizations, however, often lack a leveraging ability. This is primarily due to lack of effective coordination among various distinct IT groups and business units. One of the objectives of a COE organization should be to resolve this issue. COE delivery must involve a horizontal strategy that cuts across IT groups' boundaries and business units to ensure satisfactory client-advocacy service.

The horizontal strategy should be a coordinated set of goals and policies across the interrelated IT groups of the delivery chain. It should not replace or eliminate the need for COE distinct groups. However, it should provide explicit coordination among IT groups and end users to harmonize delivery.

Key IT end-to-end processes include service definition and marketing, service planning and deployment, service-level management, change management, and problem management. Furthermore, automated low-level processes, such as performance and capacity management, cost management, configuration management, and availability management, will be used to supplement the key processes.

What Processes Are Included in COEs?

COEs should correspond to what customers perceive to be the most valuable and important support services within data center operations.

As an operations organization moves from task to process to COE service delivery models, it needs a high-level road map. Analytical tools that can help define rewards as well as short- and long-term investments are also useful.

These analytics provide a framework that enables the following:

- A high level of reorganization governance
- Proof points for continued investment
- Rational disengagement points based on evolving business, technology, and personnel changes

While an analytical reorganization framework provides the operations organization with proof points for communications and marketing messages, more importantly it forces operations to define investments, transition plans, and critical timelines.

Most operations reorganizations ultimately fail because operations groups underestimate the time needed to demonstrate already marketed customer value. When making the transition to a COE delivery format, analytics will be a key contributing success factor, simply because operations groups can plan the work and work the plan. It is not surprising that an analytical framework does not only supply ROI estimates; it also exposes potential customer value points, which are important in improving customer relations and generating value.

Moving toward more integrated, bundled product delivery has its benefits. Although end to end, speed, adaptability, and so forth are key elements of COEs, operations groups must be aware that the selling point for COEs over typical process-based organizations will be more incremental but sustainable improvement—not always an easy sell. The move from task to process has historically provided significant efficiencies—often double-digit annual improvements for a maximum of two to three years. However, the move to COEs often results in merely incremental, but sustainable, single-digit annual operational changes (over processes). From a less quantifiable perspective, process bundling also enables operations groups to offer users bigger fish to catch.

Experiential data indicates that transitions to more bundled COE delivery models generally take less than two years for most customers. In fact, as Figure 4.2 implies, planning for longer generally produces less

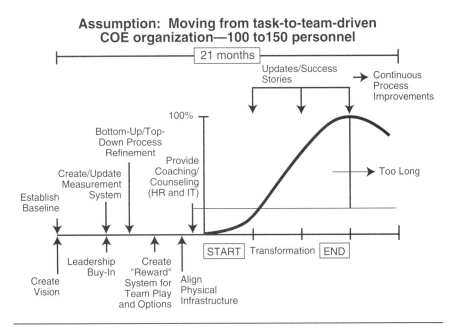

Figure 4.2 Task-to-Team COE Timeline

positive results because most users just "want to be done." However, three to nine months before the actual personnel transition, major groundwork has been accomplished. Steps such as vision creation or coaching for personnel moving to more amorphous team-like COE structures—or process groups if the organization is task-driven—are important and must be part of the solution. Process bundling requires a shared effort between HR and operations groups, with operations staff providing the lion's share of the effort.

Technology does not stand still; the same can be said for operations and organizations. As with most entities, organizations either get better or get worse: They rarely stay the same. So, trying to estimate benefits and payback time frames of organizational improvements is akin to intercepting future technology successes—never easy. Benefits are a moving target, so operations groups must build and track to a moving baseline to determine whether operations groups are getting more efficient, versus the typical do-nothing-but-focus case.

The challenge is simple: A major reorganization effort must beat the best-case, do-nothing-but-focus solution. In most cases, COEs can show 10 percent per year changes for extended periods, but before declaring victory, operations must include the personnel startup factors. Reorganizations do not happen in a vacuum, and it is often the better part of one to two years before things settle down and groups can fully exploit the inherent value of COEs (see Figure 4.3). In fact, the best-case scenario is that the reorganizing team does not lose any ground to its do-nothing-but-focus competitors.

An operations organization in transition is likely to lose some productivity during the first six to twelve months by two to five percentage points because of personnel unrest. Best-case solutions show breakeven results in less than 18 to 24 months. Although considerable emotion is associated with reorganizations, equally strong operational organization modeling energy must enable operations to develop realistic goals and solutions that provide real value—not just change for change's sake.

Eventually, this sort of reorganizational transition framework will be standard procedure, much like manufacturing organizational and production methodologies already used. More important, as the operations organization implements obvious COEs and is left with less obvious bundling alternatives—COE ROIs are more difficult to resolve—a strong analysis framework can help drive better bundling decisions. However, bundled process evolution, driven in part by operations groups' entrepreneurial vigor, will have definite long-term effects on service delivery.

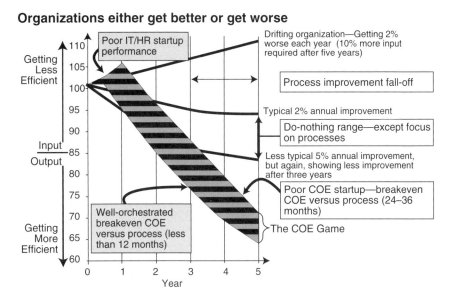

Figure 4.3 Breakeven Time Test

Quite simply, operations groups now part of the business landscape will realize that servicing evolving customers will require an annual house-cleaning, jettisoning low value-added processes.

As a result of instituting strong planning and execution for reorganizing operations groups, execution efficiencies are often five to ten percentage points per year better than typical ad hoc reorganizations. Although they intuitively accept bundled delivery as an improved organization solution, operations groups must carefully evaluate time frames, ROI, and the value that process bundling delivers.

What Products/Services Are Included within the COE?

In addition to the analytical models outlined previously, which can be used to determine ROI and timelines for COE reorganization, operations organizations also should use some basic organizational techniques to determine what products and services ultimately should be included within the COE. Doing so involves the following elements:

Research

■ Identify core competencies within the operations organization.

- Use the 80/20 rule to identify customer needs.
- Use areas of overlap to represent the main products.

Focus

- Decide what trade-offs to make—the COE can't do it all.
- Keep services process-based and narrowly focused.
- Avoid service on the "fringes," which dilutes service quality.

Define

- Document the services portfolio.
- Keep product listings very concise.
- Don't be afraid to say no.

No organization can be a panacea in terms of breadth of service support within a COE. Organizations must create finite boundaries for support. Where business requirements demand services outside of the scope of the COEs, the choice is to rapidly assimilate these capabilities or price them separately (one-off), which could include use of adjunct services (out-tasking) to complete them.

Aggregating Processes

The COE approach places an increased level of management responsibility on your operations organization. It requires both relationship management skills as well as the basic ability to render the delivery seamless from a customer perspective.

Process aggregation should tie related processes together as well as define the organizational boundaries for each COE. In addition, it shifts the focus of staff members from processes—a necessary step in the evolutionary process—to "process seams." Most operational failures occur within the seams between processes and organizations, where the handoffs occur.

Viewing each of the processes associated with each domain/platform (desktop, network, distributed computing environment, or host) reveals the several common areas that exist. Grouping these based on their logical relationship yields the fabric of each COE. (See Figure 4.4.)

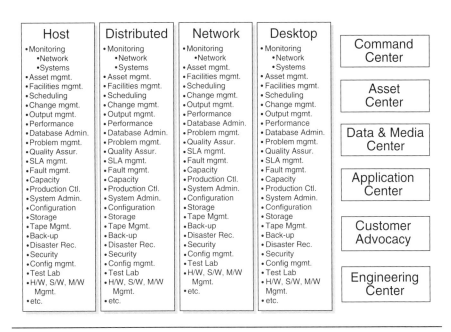

Host	Distributed	Network	Desktop
• Monitoring	• Monitoring	• Monitoring	• Monitoring
•Network	•Network	•Network	•Network
•Systems	•Systems	• Asset mgmt.	•Systems
• Asset mgmt.	• Asset mgmt.	• Facilities mgmt.	• Asset mgmt.
• Facilities mgmt.	• Facilities mgmt.	• Scheduling	• Facilities mgmt.
• Scheduling	• Scheduling	• Change mgmt.	• Scheduling
• Change mgmt.	• Change mgmt.	• Output mgmt.	• Change mgmt.
• Output mgmt.	• Output mgmt.	• Performance	• Output mgmt.
• Performance	• Performance	• Database Admin.	• Performance
• Database Admin.	• Database Admin.	• Problem mgmt.	• Database Admin.
• Problem mgmt.	• Problem mgmt.	• Quality Assur.	• Problem mgmt.
• Quality Assur.	• Quality Assur.	• SLA mgmt.	• Quality Assur.
• SLA mgmt.	• SLA mgmt.	• Fault mgmt.	• SLA mgmt.
• Fault mgmt.	• Fault mgmt.	• Capacity	• Fault mgmt.
• Capacity	• Capacity	• Production Ctl.	• Capacity
• Production Ctl.	• Production Ctl.	• System Admin.	• Production Ctl.
• System Admin.	• System Admin.	• Configuration	• System Admin.
• Configuration	• Configuration	• Storage	• Configuration
• Storage	• Storage	• Tape Mgmt.	• Storage
• Tape Mgmt.	• Tape Mgmt.	• Back-up	• Tape Mgmt.
• Back-up	• Back-up	• Disaster Rec.	• Back-up
• Disaster Rec.	• Disaster Rec.	• Security	• Disaster Rec.
• Security	• Security	• Config mgmt.	• Security
• Config mgmt.	• Config mgmt.	• Test Lab	• Config mgmt.
• Test Lab	• Test Lab	• H/W, S/W, M/W	• Test Lab
• H/W, S/W, M/W Mgmt.	• H/W, S/W, M/W Mgmt.	Mgmt.	• H/W, S/W, M/W Mgmt.
• etc.	• etc.	• etc.	• etc.

| Command Center |
| Asset Center |
| Data & Media Center |
| Application Center |
| Customer Advocacy |
| Engineering Center |

Figure 4.4 Process Aggregation

A COE model results in five or six major organizational areas and fewer units of work—six super processes instead of more than 30 separate processes.

In addition to process inter-relationships, COEs should be thought of in terms of representing:

■ Critical mass from an organizational and value-proposition perspective

■ Areas of expertise, either now or future, that have a balance of responsibility and authority

■ Opportunities for leverage by combining the staff, tools, and procedures of each process within the COE

In Table 4.2, the processes defined in Chapter 2 are mapped into their logical COEs.

Table 4.2 Process-to-COE Mapping

Process	COE
Application optimization	Application
Asset management	Asset
Budget management	Asset
Business continuity	DMC
Business relationship management	CAC
Capacity management	ESC
Change management	Shared
Configuration management	Shared
Contract management	Asset
Contractor management	Asset
Cost recovery management	Asset
Database administration (physical)	DMC
Disk storage management	ESC
Facilities management	Shared
Hardware support	ESC
Infrastructure planning	ESC
Inventory management	Asset
Job scheduling	Application
Middleware management	ESC
Negotiation management	Asset
Network monitoring	Command
Output management	DMC
Performance management	Command
Physical database management	DMC
Problem management	CAC
Production acceptance	Application
Production control	Application
Quality assurance	Application
Security management	Shared

Table 4.2 Process-to-COE Mapping *(continued)*

Process	COE
Service-level management	CAC
Service-level agreement management	CAC
Service request management	CAC
Software distribution	Application
Software management	ESC
Systems monitoring	Command
Tape management	DMC
Test lab management	ESC
Workload monitoring	Command

The Result: COEs

The key ingredients to developing a successful COE organizational model include time, patience, process focus, and loose boundaries between technical, operational, and administrative/support groups. Adopting these ingredients will be a prerequisite to excellence, and the results must have built-in continuous improvement and speed.

The final outcome of a process-driven organization includes technology, skills and staffing, best practices, metrics, and "fit" that are all defined independent of the staff that serves it. The "pieces" or tasks that constitute each process are about 80 percent generic and 20 percent idiosyncratic.

In addition, areas of core technical expertise by platform often remain. For example, fault management and detailed configuration skills will always be needed for major computing platforms, networks, and so on. Sometimes these highly technical skills are aggregated into a technical-support COE, although cultural boundaries between platforms are most difficult to surmount at this technical level.

Your operations organization *must not* be considered in a vacuum that is independent of the rest of IT. Therefore, supplementary centers of excellence have been added that may or may not be part of IT operations. For example, Figure 4.5 shows how customer advocacy, security, on-boarding, change management, mergers and acquisitions might be included. The key is that the IT operations group is represented in these centers.

Finally, some processes can coordinate efforts across center-of-excellence boundaries. For example, performance management is a process that is often staffed by a combination of staff from numerous centers and overseen by an overall performance manager. We have seen similar approaches used for quality assurance and change management.

Core COEs

Centers of excellence that are core to IT operations tend to be:

- Command center
- Asset center
- Data/media center
- Application center

The Result: Centers of Excellence

Possible COEs

| Security | Outsourcing | Change Mgmt. | Mergers & Acquisitions | Etc. |

Command Center	Asset Center	Data/Media Center	Application Center	Engineering Center	Customer Advocacy
• Network	• Inventory	• Disk	• Production Control	• Test Lab	• Problems
• System Monitoring	• Contracts	• Tape	• Job Sched.	• Infrastructure Planning	• SLAs
• Workload Monitoring	• Licensing	• Business Continuity	• Application Optimizing	• HW, SW	• BRM
• Perf. Mgmt.	• Cost Recovery	• Output		• Middleware	• Service Requests
	• Budget	• Physical Database		• Database Admin.	• Marketing
				• Capacity	

Facilities, HR, Change(?), and Configuration Management

Host	Distributed	Network	Desktop
• Fault Mgmt.	• Fault Mgmt.	• Fault Mgmt.	• Trouble-shooting
• PSI	• Design	• Configs	

Stovepipe Orientation Required (For Now)

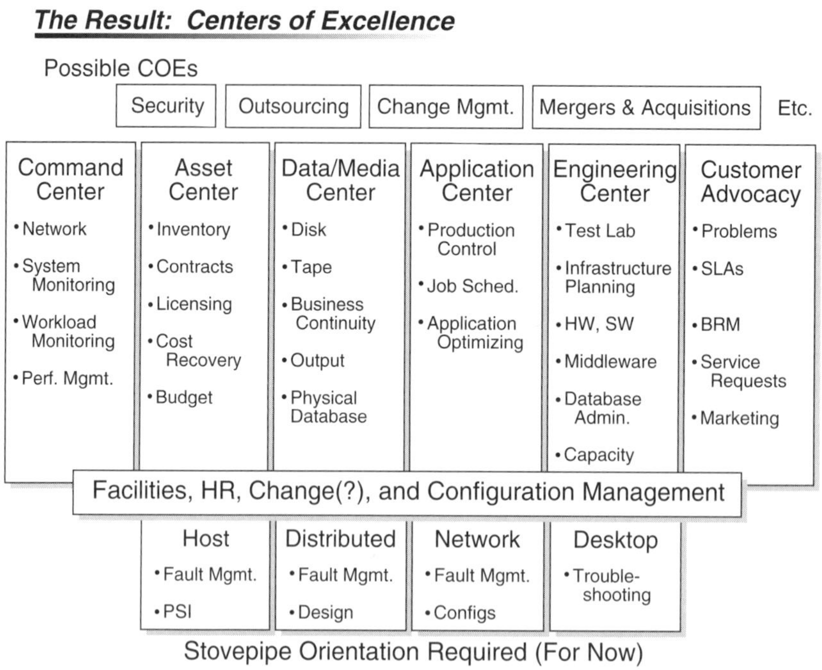

Figure 4.5 Resulting COEs

Command COE Characteristics

A command COE differs from a simple network or systems operation center in some key respects. A typical NOC or SOC employs adequate processes and automation, but its limited scope greatly reduces its value. A command COE, with its broader coverage and focus on operational processes, exploits common automation technology across silos. The result is greater economies of scale that translate into ROI. A command COE is better aligned with the business, and thus is viewed as a contributor to the bottom line. In addition to basic requirements such as strong physical security, 24×365 operation, and fault-tolerant support systems, some important factors to the success of a command COE include the following characteristics:

- *Standard, efficient, repeatable, and clustered processes with cohesive linkages.* Nothing is more important to IT operations than proper processes. This focus is particularly imperative in the command COE, where monitoring processes affiliated with fault and performance management are fundamental. Escalation and rapid-response processes react to detected incidents. Process clusters unify operational functions across silos. Fault and performance incidents are collected from all components and services within the enterprise. By implementing comprehensive coverage, root-cause identification is simpler, resulting in quicker service restoration. Configuration information clarifies the relationships that assist in root-cause identification. Processes should be generic enough to cover multiple situations. This standardization saves costs, because process exceptions force inefficient use of human capital. In fact, exception handling should follow its own robust process to minimize firefighting. Firefighting generally reflects a costly breakdown in structured processes.

- *Infrastructure and asset management technology to automate process execution.* Once the operational processes have been identified and characterized, management technology should be investigated as a means to automate these processes. A command COE uses extensive automation to monitor the infrastructure, identify anomalous incidents, assist in the escalation of incidents, and facilitate rapid response. Technology also helps measure operational performance, such as mean time to repair (MTTR). The reverse order of tool adoption should never be attempted. Trying to build processes around a chosen technology solution is almost a guaranteed failure.

- *Continual reassessment for iterative efficiency.* By collecting operational metrics to measure the performance of the command COE, all processes and technology solutions can be re-evaluated for possible improvement. This process should be continual to ensure ongoing efficiency enhancements. An elementary pursuit of the command COE is an obsession for efficiency optimization (see Figure 4.6).

- *Tight integration with the help desk.* The help desk and command COE form a tight partnership. Incidents processed by the command COE can be escalated through the help desk for resolution. The technology typically used by help desk personnel is well

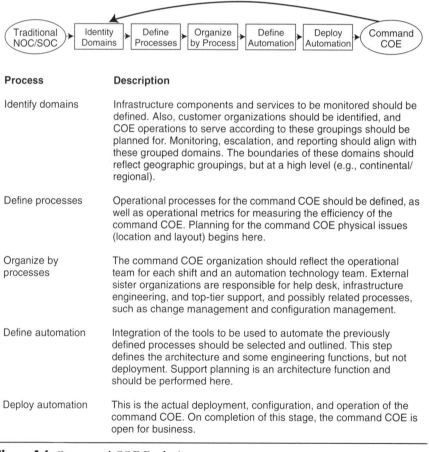

Process	Description
Identify domains	Infrastructure components and services to be monitored should be defined. Also, customer organizations should be identified, and COE operations to serve according to these groupings should be planned for. Monitoring, escalation, and reporting should align with these grouped domains. The boundaries of these domains should reflect geographic groupings, but at a high level (e.g., continental/regional).
Define processes	Operational processes for the command COE should be defined, as well as operational metrics for measuring the efficiency of the command COE. Planning for the command COE physical issues (location and layout) begins here.
Organize by processes	The command COE organization should reflect the operational team for each shift and an automation technology team. External sister organizations are responsible for help desk, infrastructure engineering, and top-tier support, and possibly related processes, such as change management and configuration management.
Define automation	Integration of the tools to be used to automate the previously defined processes should be selected and outlined. This step defines the architecture and some engineering functions, but not deployment. Support planning is an architecture function and should be performed here.
Deploy automation	This is the actual deployment, configuration, and operation of the command COE. On completion of this stage, the command COE is open for business.

Figure 4.6 Command COE Evolution

equipped for automated dispatching to the appropriate responders. It offers common mechanisms and processes for responding to automated events as well as manual events received by telephone or e-mail. If designed properly, the escalation and dispatching of automated events rarely requires the intervention of help desk staff.

Asset COE Characteristics

Better financial management disciplines within the IT organization drive business metrics, more realistic service-level agreements, and ultimately an effective IT value equation. Rigorous financial management disciplines define the efficiency and ultimately the success of the evolving service-centric IT organization. An effective, centralized asset COE headed by the IT organization's own CFO delivers the required rapid, accurate financial impact analysis and P-and-L-like accountability.

Although the IT asset COE should eventually manage all enterprise IT assets—hardware, software, contracts, and, even in some cases, the most critical human capital assets—early, quantifiable, and highly visible victories are gained most easily in the software arena. When uncontained, software budgets threaten to appropriate fully half the IT data center budget. Indeed, the urgency to establish an asset center in general and effective enterprise software asset management specifically is highlighted by these projected budget curves; shaving a few percentage points off users' near-term software budget growth can have a dramatic and lasting long-term effect. For example, during a 10-year economic horizon (realistic for software), a 15 percent annual growth yields a quadrupling of the user's current budget, while reducing that annual rate by only three points, or to 12 percent, reduces the out-year growth by 25 percent, or to 3 times the current budget.

We have grouped enterprise software asset management functions into six major groups or "buckets" that should form the foundation for the evolving asset COE. These functional groups will draw skills from many areas outside the traditional asset management purview—for example, capacity planning, legal, technical support, and operations. Most important, the software asset management organization must work and be closely integrated with corporate finance and business functions.

■ *Asset Inventory.* The adage "garbage in, garbage out" is fundamental to the effective management of enterprise software assets. Most users have difficulty identifying mainframe software assets within the data center, while distributed and open systems, especially the desktop, have deteriorated into an unmanageable challenge for software asset management. The scope and complexity of this task demands that it be automated as soon as possible.

■ *Comprehensive Cost Analysis.* Users must understand the true cost of software (including prerequisite tools, utilities, training, skills, and so on) during a realistic time frame. Moreover, these raw software costs must then be tied to the delivered business value, allowing the business to dynamically adjust priorities. For example, when the $500 thousand system that once served 100 users now has only 10, can it be eliminated?

■ *Displacement.* Fundamental to effective cost containment is a credible long-term displacement strategy. Prerequisite to the credibility of such a displacement strategy is the intimate involvement of technical support, which must provide technical analysis of current versus alternative product feature/function and feasibility and resource requirements of migration.

■ *Contracts and Terms and Conditions (Ts&Cs).* Increasingly considered one of the IT organization's key assets, existing contracts' Ts&Cs must be carefully evaluated and compared to those of new vendor bids, especially important when an incumbent vendor is acquired. The skills and experience required for effective contract analysis must be centralized within the IT group's asset center.

■ *Negotiations.* Users cannot afford to let increasingly sophisticated, aggressive software vendors negotiate strategic product procurements with anyone but a skilled, experienced, and centralized team within the IT organization's asset center.

■ *Planning.* Perhaps the most important strategic function within the asset center, planning is the "What if..." group that can have a significant impact on the long-term costs of a given project. While most IT capacity planning personnel see themselves exclusively focused on hardware, their close collaboration with the software asset management group often defines success or failure for a project's long-term total cost of ownership. Innumerable cases of software capacity caps have gone awry, costing users huge sums, often more than $1 million, because of the minimal involvement of capacity planners.

Data–and–Media COE

The Data–and–Media (D&M) COE mission is to support enterprise data in a cost-effective manner while maintaining data integrity, availability, and security. Skills within the D&M COE must include all forms of media management, such as disk, tape, and print. The value proposition is in providing common, cross-platform services.

In business terms, the value of the D&M COE can be measured by business opportunities enabled by adaptability, revenue/profitability contributions from information aggregation, and enabling systems to become more change-tolerant.

D&M COE best practices are defined by heterogeneous shared services. Management tools must be evaluated on the basis of their ability to provide a common interface and platform independence, as well as to support dynamic data categorization. Very few technology managers are aware of the residual benefits of structuring and supporting data around patterns—availability, business continuity, cost, performance, capacity, for example. These patterns enable the operations group to make better technology decisions that are guided by business requirements rather than a "one size fits all" approach.

Like all COEs, the D&M COE must also integrate with production acceptance processes. Technology managers must first leverage existing enterprise infrastructure and evolve from a reactive, request-based organization to business-driven proactive service provider. Functionally, the following five processes define the D&M COE responsibilities.

■ *Disk storage management* includes:

  - Usage of storage resources should be optimized.

  - Granular service levels based on business need and data criticality should be offered.

  - Policies for disk management should be defined.

  - Capacity must be balanced against demand.

  - Backup/recovery should be provided.

  - Storage hardware and interconnect should be managed.

  - Performance should be improved through data classification.

  - Storage technologies (such as SAN, NAS, Fiber Channel) should be assessed and exploited.

  - Emerging storage technologies (such as iSCSI, CoD, Gigabit Ethernet) should be evaluated.

- *Tape management* includes:
  - Methods to allocate, store, administer, and optimize tape usage should be managed.
  - Automated tape technology should be exploited.

- *Output management* includes:
  - Delivery of computer-generated output to appropriate distribution target (device or user) should be managed.
  - Number of physical outputs should be optimized/reduced.

- *Physical database management* includes:
  - Physical design allocation of database systems.
  - Optimization and physical database recovery processes.

- *Business continuity* includes:
  - Continuous availability of contingent business processes should be ensured as required by the business.
  - Business continuity strategies and tactics should be optimized.
  - Recovery requirements for business applications (regardless of platform/network) should be identified and documented.
  - Backup/archival processes for critical data should be managed.
  - Recovery processes should be tested.

The D&M COE should be tightly integrated with asset management processes to ensure conformity and standardization. Asset COE constituents will need critical business and technical information to support procurement processes seeking to leverage aggregation of purchasing power to eliminate costly over-purchase practices. Many organizations continue to procure media solutions in a stovepiped fashion and fail to account for integration and support inefficiencies. Research has consistently shown that proper communication of requirements to asset COE constituents yields lower total cost of ownership through support rationalization.

Application COE Characteristics

The goal of an application center of excellence is both to manage the full business application portfolio effectively (such as ERP, best in class, legacy) and to minimize the required use of outside consultants on future projects.

The application COE (ACOE) is responsible for designing, building, and running commercial business applications for the organization. The ACOE's prime responsibility is to train and support a variety of end users: super-users, heads-down users, casual users, reporting/analytic users, Web-based users—including suppliers and customers—across ERP, best-in-class, and legacy systems as well as interoperability among application classes. The ACOE acts as an internal systems integrator, providing both staffing and methodology for new business automation efforts, with a centricity on ERP. The ACOE works closely with other key IT organizational units.

It adopts the corporate philosophy that strategy drives architecture, architecture supports continuous business change, and, therefore, new business applications must integrate with the overall architecture. Consequently, both ACOE and the IT architecture strategy group play key roles in application selection and implementation. Both groups work together to define the approach toward new applications with existing infrastructure in areas such as middleware and interoperability, security, distributed systems management, and data warehouse/data mart architecture.

The ACOE maintains development, test, and production systems that logically, if not physically, support new user requirements, bug fixes, new releases from package vendors, and so forth. This requires obvious alignment with version control and software configuration management. The ACOE may maintain a small cadre of DBAs to manage the ongoing tuning of the applications. It ensures that new business applications are instrumented well to support an operation's ongoing performance analysis.

ACOE Job Functions

Business Strategy/Subject-Matter Experts. The ACOE works with line-of-business (LOB) executives to make the business case for new commercial business applications and agree on the key metrics of quantified benefits (perhaps framed as ROI, economic value, and the like), total cost of ownership, and time to benefit. ACOE subject-matter experts (in areas such as finance, manufacturing, and logistics) work on cross-functional business process teams and provide high-level support for end users in production.

Application Implementation Infrastructure. The ACOE deploys project-management software and provides project leadership for new initiatives. (This is a major shortcoming in many client organizations, and outside training should be considered.) The ACOE develops an application implementation methodology, creating alignment with the respective methodologies of the application package vendor and the systems integrator (SI). It develops a groupware approach for knowledge sharing through all phases of the application life cycle. This capability is well understood by systems integrators, and IT organizations should insist on knowledge transfer here as a key component of an SI contract. The ACOE adopts the version control/software configuration management techniques used for internal application development.

Change Management, Training, Help Desk. The ACOE develops expertise in helping to introduce change to end-user organizations that are often reluctant. Training must be coordinated, both for IT staff and end users, and the ACOE will engage outside trainers as it develops a set of software standards for managing the training functions. In particular, new ERP implementations will put undue strain on the help desk, and the ACOE is responsible for coordinating LOB users, help desk staff, and IT specialists to provide ongoing support of new applications. The ACOE also manages the continuing flow of documentation from the package vendors, as well as ongoing customization.

Product/Technical Expertise. For large business applications, the ACOE maintains a skill base in areas such as configuration, custom coding, workflow, and decision support, to be able to populate new teams for ongoing development. On the technical side, the ACOE supports a small group of technical experts in areas such as database administration, networking, and distributed systems management, primarily as liaison to existing infrastructure groups within IT departments.

COE Staff

The two unique aspects of the COE organization, from a personnel standpoint, are the COE "brain trust" and the *rapid-response team* (RRT). These two groups, by definition, comprise the most powerful and knowledgeable staff. The brain trust focuses on process/COE improvement. The RRT covers assimilation of new workloads.

The COE Brain Trust

Within each COE, the "brain trust" comprises the best and brightest technical and operational staff, with a charter to provide the analysis and improvements necessary to achieving and maintaining excellence. These same staff often participate in rapid assimilation response teams, whether through direct involvement or through development of standard tools/checklists to ensure that the requirements of operations groups are met. Ultimately, the roles that these staff carry out are critical in three ways:

- Insulating core staff and work teams from change
- Establishing and maintaining excellence in all related processes
- Determining the future of how the center will provide value to customers

As mentioned earlier, within a given COE, 10 to 20 percent of staff represent the general COE management, analyzing and improving the many processes contained within the COE and, perhaps more importantly, managing the seams between one COE and another.

COE groups can range in size from a few people in smaller organizations to 30 or more in very large companies. The principles are the same, however, in that COEs tend to leverage staff better and provide opportunities for cross training and career advancement at a much higher level than most current organizations, which are structured around stovepipe, plan/build/run, or projects.

The COE RRT

Every IT organization needs a rapid-assimilation group focused on providing insight regarding the minimum requirements for production acceptance, coupled with a response team armed with devices such as a gap analysis, matrix of processes, and quick-hit checklist (see Figure 4.7) that translates business needs into operational support requirements. The value domain signals the success in key organizational objectives in the metrics that are used to report IT results. The strategy domain will be addressed primarily through the customer advocacy COE, where the business relationship manager will be used to convey IT offerings while providing a single point of control for obtaining IT services.

Spawning RRTs from COEs ensures that the core delivery teams are insulated from change to support existing workloads, as well as ensuring early and proactive involvement in business initiatives to the point that the connection becomes nearly real time. As the role of these teams evolves during the next two to three years, the accelerated life cycle of business and IT operations groups will relegate RRTs to virtual teams, driven by staff members within the application center who are focused on production acceptance.

Technology Domain	Availability (Fault Management)	Capacity Planning	Cost (Contracts)	Systems Administration	Backup/ Disaster Recovery
Host/Server					
Middleware					
Network					
Desktop Footprint					

Map Platforms across Processes/Functions/Criteria

Figure 4.7 New Application Quick-Hit Matrix

Rapid Assimilation

COEs not only have to organize existing processes, they also must absorb new applications, departments, or even entire organizations added via merger or acquisition. Ideally, business units, departmental IT groups, application development, and early initiators would involve infrastructure and operational specialists to perform impact assessments and prepare for the new business changes (applications) that are occurring.

Then the application, any new or changed infrastructure, and new or modified operational procedures could occur in tandem—and the formal production acceptance process would be a given.

Likewise, in a perfect world, operations development and the application development lifecycle will be closely integrated in a bi-directional fashion. However, time and business realities preclude such extensive integration in most organizations. Although most operations organizations learn to address manageability and supportability requirements over the longer term, the short-term reality usually involves condensed rapid assimilation procedures executed at the implementation phase.

As mentioned in the previous section, RRTs spawned from various COEs can use various tools to translate business needs into operational requirements. What's needed is a way to map those operational requirements to predefined constructs that will expedite the support of these new endeavors.

Another book in this series, *The Adaptive Enterprise: IT Infrastructure Strategies to Manage Change and Enable Growth,* offers a detailed process for infrastructure development. Central to that process is the idea of "patterns," which are complete predesigned end-to-end solutions that can be molded simply and quickly to fit the latest business requirements. By identifying and creating a series of reusable infrastructure patterns, you will be prepared to handle most of the application requests that come your way faster, cheaper, and better.

Common patterns (see Figure 4.8) and pattern-oriented thinking can simplify your own infrastructure planning and make application development easier.

The infrastructure necessary for a given application is determined by who uses it and how they use it. Since users interact with applications in only a small number of ways, and applications interact with other applications in a similarly small number of ways, it is not difficult to describe an application by the types of interactions it employs, and thus its infrastructure requirements.

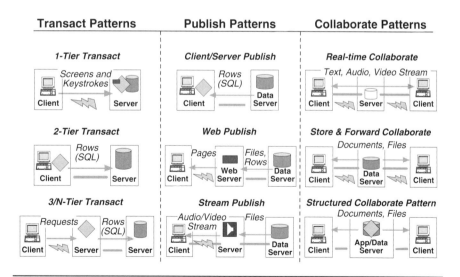

Figure 4.8 The Nine Basic Patterns

While no organization should expect to run all their enterprise applications on a single IT infrastructure, it is impractical and inefficient to allow networks, hardware, software, and business processes to grow unchecked with separate decisions and implementations each time an application is deployed.

The adaptive infrastructure patterns outlined here have evolved to reduce many possible infrastructure options to a small number of descriptive archetypes, so they may be used to plan for simplified and reusable infrastructure configurations.

Patterns are the information, insight, and experience—the "what is" and "how to"—that are common to an existing class of applications. This information is captured in a form that makes it easier to reuse with future applications of the same class. Patterns also capture experience and best practices for projects that result from real application requests by the business, and they emphasize end-to-end reuse in a logical rather than a physical way.

Reusability is the key to making patterns effective. Once you've designed a successful application using a full spectrum of infrastructure components, you can use most (if not all) of that experience to design, build, deploy, and run the next application that needs similar resources. For example, after you figure out how a mainframe application runs on mainframe infrastructure, you can deploy other mainframe applications on the same infrastructure much more quickly and efficiently.

Approximately 80 to 90 percent of all infrastructure needs can be accommodated consistently by a set of fewer than 10 patterns. Although the specifics of these patterns may change to accommodate new technologies, and certainly will differ in detail from company to company, the number of patterns needed is almost always relatively small.

The practical goal when identifying patterns is to accommodate basic differences between applications. So keep in mind the 80/20 rule and leave the last 20 percent of the differences outside of the standards. In other words, pick patterns that apply to most of the work, get them designed, and then get to using them—that's the real benefit.

How are patterns determined? While this is covered in more detail in *The Adaptive Enterprise,* you can start by asking the key questions:

- Who are the users?
- Where are they located?
- What kind of work do they need to accomplish?

In many cases, patterns may be differentiated simply by asking "what?" For example, two-way real-time collaboration is a completely different kind of activity from taking orders that a user keys into a system. On the other hand, many transactional applications can run on all three of the Transact patterns we define. The deciding factor on which Transact pattern to use might be service-level requirements, quality of service requirements, or cost restraints.

Today, nine starter patterns are recognized. They cover three basic interaction types:

- Transact patterns: Applications in which business data is written and stored for a long period of time, such as online customer orders and other transactions.

- Publish patterns: Applications with read-only data, such as online marketing information.

- Collaborate patterns: Applications where information contained in files and documents is shared between two or more users, such as a product design document shared by a development team.

Figure 4.8 provides a set of thumbnail diagrams showing how each of the patterns work, and the following text provides a brief description of each. For a more detailed explanation, please see *The Adaptive Enterprise*.

The 1-Tier Transact Pattern

This pattern includes batch processing applications or online transaction processing (OLTP) applications without logical abstraction between the presentation, application, and data logic. Although the application itself is fully centralized, users may be widely distributed over wide-area networks (WANs).

The 2-Tier Transact Pattern

This pattern involves a "smart PC" on the desktop communicating directly with a back-end database server. This includes Web servers that intertwine CGI/ASP/JSP presentation and application logic. This is the quickest and cheapest Transact pattern from a development perspective. However, it has several major drawbacks, making it largely unsuitable outside of a workgroup. Scalability issues limit it to small-scale OLTP workloads. Additionally, the heavy integration of application logic and screen presentation logic makes application-to-application integration extremely difficult.

This category includes most of the traditional client/server applications that became popular earlier in the 1990s and are still popular today, albeit veiled by browser front-end. Common examples of 2-Tier transaction pattern-based applications include those programmed in Visual Basic or PowerBuilder, and most Web applications using Microsoft active server pages (ASP) or Java server pages (JSP).

The 3/N-Tier Transact Pattern

This pattern consists of a thin client carrying presentation-logic only, communicating with a client-neutral, server-based application, which in turn communicates with a back-end database server. Common examples include Peoplesoft v8 and SAP R/3, especially version 4.6 or later.

With a Web server, the presentation is generated on another Web server tier, yet rendered still by the Web browser. This is truly an N-tier rather than just a traditional 3-Tier design. Because most applications are using this technique, there is no point in planning 3-Tier separately from N-Tier. Thus, the Starter Kit pattern provided in this chapter is defined as 3/N-Tier.

The 3/N-Tier Transact pattern is the most scalable and flexible client/server transaction pattern. Due to the WAN-friendliness of the client-to-application server protocols, users can be highly decentralized. When implemented correctly, this pattern results in clearly defined interfaces, making it the most flexible to integrate with other applications or points of interaction.

The Client/Server Publish Pattern

This pattern is defined by the use of a smart PC (such as a sophisticated business intelligence client) with associated session-oriented protocols (such as SQLNet) inserted between the client and back-end database. This pattern is best used for implementing sophisticated data analysis capabilities for a small, well-defined user base.

This pattern differentiates itself from the other Publish patterns in terms of the amount of processing that is performed after a query is made to a database. Applications that fit this pattern are online analytical processing (OLAP) tools and reporting-intensive applications, which require a smart PC for post-query processing support. Common examples include products from Business Objects, Brio, Cognos, MicroStrategies, and SAS Institute. The Client/Server Publish pattern is the most popular Publish pattern inside the enterprise.

The Web Publish Pattern

This pattern is defined by the use of an HTML browser and HTTP protocol to enable read-only access to structured XML or HTML documents. As such, it is more flexible than the Client/Server Publish pattern in supporting large, less well-defined user groups. But it is limited in the sophistication of the read-only interactivity and analysis it can support.

This pattern is best used for read-only Web-centric access to data and content, including documents and pages, while leaving other Publish patterns to deal with other read-only content. Common examples include any type of brochure-style Web site, package tracking for overnight delivery services, and Web-based account review or bill presentation applications. Currently, this is the most popular Publish pattern for applications reaching beyond the enterprise boundaries.

The Stream Publish Pattern

This pattern is used for real-time publishing of streaming content (such as audio, video, and text, and so forth) to "multimedia player" clients such as Windows Media Player, RealAudio, etc. Although the Web Publish pattern enables playback of multimedia files, this is accomplished as a more traditional "file download." Streaming plays the file in near real time as it downloads. The latency requirements of real-time multimedia delivery are different enough that streaming requires its own pattern.

Common examples of Stream Publish include Internet radio stations and film clip Web sites. Streaming media is a centerpiece of most consumer entertainment Web sites and an increasingly valuable feature of many sites as it enhances the "stickiness" of the site.

The Real-Time Collaborate Pattern

This pattern is quite similar to the Stream Publish pattern, because both involve enabling real-time transmission of audio and video. However, because collaboration implies two-way information exchange (as opposed to the one-way flow of Stream Publishing), real-time collaboration warrants its own separate pattern.

Applications in this category use streaming audio, video, graphics, or text to share information between users. The communication can flow either through a server for scalability and to provide community interaction, or straight from peer-to-peer. Common examples include Microsoft NetMeeting, Voice Over Internet (VoIP), instant messaging (as on AOL), and any type of videoconferencing (Web-based or otherwise).

The Store-and-Forward Collaborate Pattern

This pattern involves the basic transfer, replication, and storage of files or documents. Common examples include e-mail attachments, distributed file systems, and print queues. Most organizations also put desktop support and software distribution into this pattern, because the same people who support the NOS also support the desktops (or at least the groups are very closely allied). Often, this pattern is managed by the Distributed Systems Group within IT, which may operate under many different names.

Still, this is one pattern where most organizations—perhaps unwittingly—have employed a very pattern-centric approach to planning.

The Structured Collaborate Pattern

Structured collaboration, also known as workflow or document management, provides many important integrity-checking features that are missing from the Store-and-Forward Collaborate pattern, including version control, check-in/check-out, and data validation. For this reason, it is more scalable (from a business perspective) for business use cases requiring these capabilities. But it also requires a longer implementation cycle and is several times more expensive.

This pattern includes any application that provides shared access and automated coordinated change to a document, file, or other data structure. Common examples include Lotus Notes groupware and workflow applications (except simple e-mail), document management applications, Web content management systems, many software development environments, and shared groupware calendars.

Conclusion

The evolution of organizations from task to process is a microcosm of the next level evolution: the aggregation of processes to represent a higher form of service contribution under the COE model. The simple model that saw related tasks, skills, staff, and others come together is applied to create fewer, wider-scope competencies that ensure an end-to-end purview and clearly defined service levels.

COE structures will enable business self-alignment by bringing business strategies closer to people and improving business processes to achieve higher levels of client satisfaction. This connection will lead to business managers spending less time communicating strategies to staff, employees knowing what to do and being empowered to do it, and clients being surprised and delighted with what they are getting for their IT investment.

A fully realized COE can quantify particular value propositions and service capabilities that have greater meaning to your customers. The direct translation to business value becomes the key ingredient to successful integration of your operations group with your business, sharing decision making when identifying and prioritizing business initiatives. When this occurs, the transition to an operations excellence orientation is well under way.

Chapter 5

Metrics

Since the 1950s, all theories of business quality management have stressed the importance of continuous improvement. They contend that a one-time correction by itself will not solve quality problems or significantly raise quality levels. Instead, quality improvement requires a continuously self-refining process. Such a process relies on metrics to establish where and by how much it is succeeding and where and by how much it is failing. It then applies tools to address the shortcomings.

As a result, metrics are recognized as central to the success of most quality improvement programs. For example, the CMM model for software development discussed in Chapter 1 (consult Table 1.1) expresses the fourth level in the five-level maturity model as: "Managed Process—Detailed measures of the software process and product quality are collected. Both the software process and products are quantitatively understood and controlled." This step leads directly to the final step: continuous refinement. Other quality-improvement programs, such as TQM, likewise rely heavily on metrics to form a permanent gauge of process health and quality levels.

The data streams provided by metrics are useful diagnostic tools. For the IT group, they are critical in establishing whether the group is meeting SLA service levels to users. For companies that do not use SLAs internally, metrics enable IT staff to know what it is delivering to the users.

In modern IT departments, metrics have additional roles, which make their adoption even more compelling. Metrics allow IT organizations to demonstrate their value to the larger company. The benefits of being able to do this are numerous. These include being able to answer questions such as:

- Does IT improve business performance, and if so, how and how much?

- Does the IT group perform satisfactorily in delivering a competitive advantage?

- Does the company spend enough on the IT group?

- Has the IT organization become more or less efficient in terms of the dollars it spends?

- Has the IT group improved services?

An IT organization that cannot answer these questions with clear, compelling answers is at risk. It simply does not have the factual basis for obtaining the resources, or perhaps even the respect, needed for carrying on its work satisfactorily. Likewise, it has no basis for convincing the wider organization of its value.

For IT departments to make the best use of metrics, they must track IT metrics diligently and then translate them into business metrics for their customers' use.

Pure IT Metrics

IT metrics are the raw materials of the metrics. They serve as the fundamental data source for the IT department itself. That is, much of the management of IT processes and operations relies on the metrics attached to them.

Associating metrics with specific operations allows managers to measure the efficiency of operations. With a long history of metrics, a manager can see how various aspects of a particular process are trending. Trend analysis is a valuable diagnostic tool. It tells a manager when things are not working properly or when subtle changes in workload (such as shifting customer needs) occur. Hence, a manager armed with metrics and trend analysis is optimally capable of responding quickly to changes in his environment.

In addition, by use of metrics he can identify what new resources he needs in his department; and he has the wherewithal to justify his request to management. If his knowledge of metrics is particularly deep, he can even quantify with great precision and accuracy the benefits of new resources to his department and, more importantly, to the company.

Metrics Gap Analysis

The first step in making sure an IT department is tracking the correct metrics is to perform a gap analysis. As with other gap analyses, the process starts with the compilation of an inventory of metrics that are currently being used. Table 5.1 shows a sample form for collecting this data.

Metrics should be gathered for every IT process inventoried previously in this book. After this process is complete, the inventory forms

Table 5.1 Sample Form for Inventorying IT Process Metrics

Process	Metric	Metric Frequency*
...	...	...

*Frequency refers to how often the metric is collected.

the baseline for the gap analysis. The metrics should then be compared to those listed for the corresponding process in the process catalog in Chapter 7. A list of the missing metrics should be recorded and grouped by process. This constitutes the task list for instituting new metrics.

Note that the number of metrics varies widely by process. Many processes have three or four standard metrics to track. For example, service-request management has these fairly predictable metrics:

- Number of requests per month
- Number of requests per staff
- Mean time to resolve for each request (by type)
- Number of late service events per number of requests

However, a process such as network management requires dozens of actively tracked metrics. Perhaps because network management inherently requires a large statistical basis, many managers overlook or even dismiss the importance of simple, pragmatic metrics like those associated with simpler processes. This error is dangerous. A manager who lacks the quantitative information associated with the metrics just listed for service-request management finds himself in a difficult position when arguing in favor of more staff to handle user requests. How can he justify the expense of an additional position if he does not know how much work his staff is doing, what the trend is, or how much staffs at other firms do?

In this particular example, a manager who fails to capture the metrics but who uses a logging system for requests can be saved by the system. He can generate the information, providing that the system captures all needed data, such as the date a request was received and the date it was completed. However, many metrics do not enjoy a backup data source from which historical performance can be calculated. In such cases, the failure to collect even simple metrics is almost invariably costly.

Other Aspects of IT Metrics

After IT metrics have been collected for a while, they represent a valuable database by which a department can measure its own progress. For example, Table 5.2 presents a form that all IT departments should use to establish basic metrics about the role of the IT organization within the larger company.

A key benefit of tracking this data arises from the comparison of items N and O with the corresponding items from previous years. If the

Table 5.2 Basic Metrics to Measure the Value of IT

Item	Description		Number
A.	Total revenue of corporate entities served by the IT group		
B.	Total IT budget		
C.	Total IT budget divided by IT operations		
D.	Total number of non-IT employees supported by the IT group		
E.	Total number of IT employees		
F.	Total number of IT employees in IT operations		
G.	% total revenue for IT	(B/A) * 100	
H.	% total revenue for operations	(C/A) * 100	
I.	% IT budget for operations	(C/B) * 100	
J.	% IT operations employees	(F/E) * 100	
K.	Non-IT to IT ratio	(D:E)	
L.	Non-IT to operations ratio	(D:F)	
M.	IT cost per employee	(B/D)	
N.	IT operations cost per employee	(C/D)	
O.	IT operations cost per IT operations employee	(C/F)	

trend is not declining, IT managers should know why. If they don't, they should consult other IT metrics.

The numbers generated by this form and by the metrics used in best practices should be compared to corresponding numbers at other companies. This comparison gives a company an excellent gauge of how cost-effective an IT organization is in relation to its peers.

A good overall metric to determine cost effectiveness is the percentage of a company's gross revenue that is budgeted for IT. This number varies widely by industry. The technical consulting industry, for example, tallies numbers in the upper teens, while manufacturing tends to run in the 1 to 2 percent range. So, it's important to compare figures within the same industry. Many market-analysis firms publish these numbers every year. Get fresh data for the comparison and double check previous years against your own data, so that the comparison of current year figures will be as meaningful as possible.

Mapping IT Metrics to Business Metrics

Pure IT metrics constitute the raw materials of an intelligent metrics program. They are the basis by which an IT organization can measure its own effectiveness and compare these results to past performance and future goals. However, as plain data points, IT metrics are of little value to the IT group's principal customers: users in the larger organization.

To be useful, IT metrics must be mapped to business metrics employed by the larger organization. And, for an IT department to perform this mapping, it must first learn the metrics that are important to its various customer constituencies in the firm.

Different lines of business have different business metrics that they track and rely on. For example, see Table 5.3, which shows some departments and typical metrics they might use. This table shows that different departments frequently rely on different metrics. It also illustrates another point: Even when two departments use the same metric, they may use it differently. For example, metric F—the number of orders entered per minute—is important to manufacturing because it represents a threshold for the maximum number of orders per minute that manufacturing can expect to process; whereas for the sales department, it shows how efficiently incoming orders are entered into the system.

So to use IT metrics wisely in communication with customer departments, it's necessary to understand which business metrics are important to the customer and how those metrics are used.

Table 5.3 Business Metrics and Their Use by Different Departments

Metric	Department: Metrics Used
A. # of calls serviced within 48 hours	Sales: B, C, E, F
B. Cost per sales call	Accounting: B, D,
C. # of sales calls/day	Manufacturing: D, F
D. Cost/unit manufactured	Customer Service: A, E
E. # of RFI forms filled out electronically	
F. # of orders entered per minute	

Mapping Business and IT Metrics

This process is important because customers do not care about IT metrics per se, but they do care how IT affects their business processes. For instance, IT might measure response time, whereas a business that enters customer orders by hand might want to know the maximum number of orders a clerk can enter in one hour. The department's metric is not response time, it's orders per hour, and it is up to the IT department to translate its own metrics into the business metrics when communicating between the two departments.

Likewise, service levels, as in SLAs, must reflect business value rather than only IT value. When negotiated with technically savvy departments, SLA requirements often cross over into an area where business and IT metrics look a lot alike. Metrics that express business values through IT processes are often referred to as *modified* IT metrics. They include measures such as number of minutes of down time during critical business hours, number of special requests filled by line of business per month, and so forth. These are clearly IT measures, but ones that have a direct implication for a specific line of business.

Figure 5.1 shows how metrics are chosen in many enterprises.

The goal is to map IT metrics to business metrics, understanding that in specific cases, modified IT metrics are sufficient.

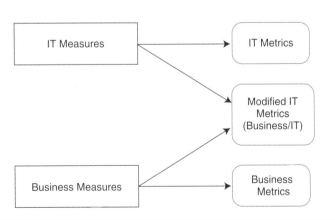

Figure 5.1 Interplay of Business and IT Metrics

To arrive at the metrics that will make the most sense, IT personnel should undertake a series of steps:

- Categorize users
  - line of business (sales, distribution, manufacturing, etc.)
  - internal/external
  - executive, middle management, and so forth
- Identify users key business metrics for each category
- Benchmark current business performance using business metrics
- Identify IT resources currently utilized to ensure business performance
- Identify which IT metrics should be tracked to gauge whether IT provides these resources at expected levels of service

Notice that the third step requires IT to benchmark a department using the department's own measures. This process enables IT personnel to see how the department sees itself. Understanding this is a key to excellent service—even quite apart from any consideration of metrics as such. Do not skip this step.

Table 5.4 shows three lists of representative metrics: IT metrics, modified IT metrics, and business metrics. They are chosen with no particular relation to each other. Each column stands by itself, but it shows the qualitative difference between each type of metric. Know your audience and which types of metrics it can best relate to.

Having examined the basic types of metrics and how they are used externally, we now examine IT metrics, whose greatest benefit accrues to the IT staff for internal management purposes.

Qualitative Metrics

Qualitative metrics occupy an important role in assessing IT operations. Because of the traditional focus on SLAs and other quantitative aspects of performance, many managers overlook the single most important statistic: How happy are customers with the IT services they receive?

The answer to this question is important. A department might be doing everything right by its SLAs and its metrics, but if customers are not satisfied, they will still complain—and IT managers need to know this.

Table 5.4 Representative Metrics Categorized by Type

IT Metrics	Modified IT Metrics	Business Metrics
Installed MIPS	System availability by application and platform	Percentage of calls serviced within 48 hours
Used MIPS	Response time by application and platform	Number of policies issued in a work day
Prime shift of percentage busy	Number of problems by severity and line of business	Cost per sales call
Installed disk storage (in GB)	Number of requests filled per month by line of business	Number of sales call per day per salesperson
Percentage of disk storage allocated	Average time to resolve level 1 and 2 problems	Income in dollars for sales per sale call
Number of tape mounts	Hardware failures by line of business	Number of orders entered per hour
...	...	...

The way to find this out is through the use of surveys. Surveys should be an integral part of a balanced IT scorecard. Surveys are difficult to perform, because formulating the questions correctly is not easy. Questions have to be clear and the forms have to be designed correctly. Here are a few tips from the book *Benchmarking*. (See Appendix A for additional information about this book.)

■ A self-administered survey should be self-explanatory. Reading instructions should not be necessary because they will not be interpreted consistently.

■ Self-administered questionnaires should be restricted to closed answers. If respondents are asked use their own words, the answers are likely to become vague. (Note: A comments section at the end of the survey can prove invaluable.)

■ The question forms in a self-administered questionnaire should be few in number. The more the questionnaire can be set up so that the respondent has the same kinds of tasks and questions to answer, the less likely it is that respondents will become confused, and the easier the task will be for them.

■ A questionnaire should be typeset and designed so that it is clear and uncluttered.

■ Provide redundant information to respondents. If people can be confused about what they are supposed to do, they will be.

■ The creative use of question formats (such as running together a string of questions that have the same answer options) and simplified data demands combined with the use of professional presentation formats help to increase the response rates.

The biggest obstacle to gathering data through surveys is undoubtedly lack of response. To drive up response so that answers are statistically valid, consider the following options:

■ Inquiries at the point of service

■ Focused face-to-face surveys

■ Periodic broad-based surveys

■ The use of incentives for response

Understanding the results of surveys is as important as formulating the questionnaire. Here are some key considerations:

■ Remember that surveys are inherently subjective and that opinions, unlike pure IT metrics, can be influenced. (But don't shy away from asking questions even when you know that the results might be negative. An effective department needs to know about all dissatisfaction.)

■ Consider overall IT surveys separately from surveys that measure response to specific functions (such as help desks, etc.)

■ Balance satisfaction with service with user assessment of the importance of the service to the business function

Survey results should corroborate quantitative IT metrics. If they do not, the divergence between the two data sets must be investigated and explained. It should not be ignored. In most cases, it suggests that the wrong metrics are being used.

Value Metrics

This chapter has examined metrics from two perspectives: 1) as a tool for demonstrating the value of IT to customers within the enterprise by mapping IT metrics to the customers' business metrics, and 2) as a measure of the efficiency and quality of internal IT operations. A third use of IT metrics enhances their value even further: IT metrics enable an IT organization to establish its value to the corporation, particularly with regard to costs. The idea is to track metrics that allow IT managers to determine the cost of IT to the company. From this base, an IT manager can act as CFOs of IT operations, knowing where things can be improved cost-wise and what the larger company's tolerance for increased investment might be.

The metrics to use in this assessment are similar to those in Table 5.2. They include:

■ IT budget as percentage of gross company revenue

■ IT operations budget as a percentage of gross company revenue

■ Trends in IT spending

■ IT to non-IT support ratios

■ IT and operations cost per employee

These data items furnish a manager with considerable information about how IT is viewed by executive management. A good manager knows how these numbers are trending and how they stack up against peer IT departments at competitors.

Performing this analysis, however, requires care in understanding the numbers under examination. For example, comparisons of IT budget as a percent of company revenue can be misleading if the company as a whole is performing poorly. As revenue drops, all cost centers become larger cost factors. Likewise, if for unusual reasons a company enjoys especially high revenue for a year, the comparison of IT to revenue will be skewed in the opposite direction. In these situations, comparing the IT costs to some other business metric may make more sense. In all cases, access to comparative historical data proves invaluable in assessing the ratio correctly.

When this exercise is performed regularly, managers are often surprised to see the prominent role played by human capital. Turnover ratios and other human-capital metrics often can be linked directly to IT performance issues. In addition, the costs of education and improving employee skills often can be quantified by these metrics. Invariably, these numbers will suggest the value of instituting a skill-transition/improvement plan for all employees.

Ongoing Metrics Reporting

Ongoing reporting of metrics is a fundamental part of IT best practices. A site that does not regularly collect metrics as part of its *daily* operations is in jeopardy of losing the benefits of quality-improvement efforts. More importantly, it risks losing control of its internal operations. As a result, managers need to plan the collection and reporting of metrics. The plan should be written to cover these four points:

- The metrics to be collected and tracked
- Reporting frequency
- Reporting vehicle
- Constituency

The first point has been discussed at length in this chapter.

Reporting frequency depends a lot on the metric involved. Some metrics, such as disk usage, should be collected on a continuous basis. Others, such as IT costs per employee, may need to be done only semi-annually. Wisdom and experience dictate frequency. However, this subjective aspect must not preclude them from being explicitly defined. Every metric in the plan should have an explicit frequency, and this frequency must be enforced.

The reporting vehicle varies widely depending on the metric. Disk usage, for example, should be reported in real time on a console and possibly on an IT intranet. It should also have a paper counterpart published periodically, say monthly, to give managers a snapshot view of trends in the department. Paper-to-Web reporting allows departments to transition from point-in-time events to a continuous reporting stream: Reports are constantly updated on the department intranet and paper reports can be printed at any time to capture a hard-copy time slice. Another advantage of posting some metrics on the intranet is to gain information about when users are looking at the system. Most customers don't care about system performance statistics except when processing is slow or frozen. So, sudden surges in interest are almost always symptomatic of a problem. Numerous packages enable sites to track and monitor site usage, so spikes in viewership can be captured in real time and diagnostic work can begin immediately.

The audience is the final factor conditioning a reporting system. Much of this chapter has discussed how users view IT metrics different from the IT staff. Reporting methods likewise are conditioned by the role of the ultimate consumer of the information. Data published outside the department should be cast into the appropriate business metrics. The metrics plan should state explicitly the mapping between business metrics and the constituent IT metrics. For an audience of senior executives, IT managers can do well by preparing an "IT Annual Report" (consult Chapter 6), which presents many of the metrics discussed in the previous section on value metrics. This annual report demonstrates the value and the cost of IT to senior executives. It helps them appreciate the importance of IT problems and the value of IT successes. It is good public relations for the department.

Metrics enable IT departments to recognize and diagnose problems early, monitor trends in their operations, enforce quality-improvement programs, present themselves effectively to outside customers, and argue persuasively for resources to executive management. Few other activities available to an IT organization bring such rich and continuous benefits.

Chapter 6

Putting It All Together

In addition to attaining operational efficiency, IT organizations must focus on quality of service and customer satisfaction. Few IT organizations have the broad vision that integrates the following functions and enables executives to manage delivery of IT services as a value chain—that is, to deliver IT services as an integrated set that is measured by its impact on the end user:

- *SLAs*, including understanding end-user requirements, setting expectations for services provided, tracking actual performance, and reporting results to appropriate constituencies. By 2003, estimates state about 60 percent of IT organizations will have functioning SLAs, but not until 2005 or 2006 will a majority of IT managers be compensated according to performance in these SLAs.

- *Service productization*, including the definition of standard "products" within the various IT organizations, the service levels for each product, and the prices charged to end users for them. Roughly 35 percent of Global 2000 IT organizations currently have productized services, although quality remains inconsistent and usage-based charge-back is limited to approximately 20 percent of IT organizations.

- *BRM*, including the organizational structure, daily responsibilities, methods for understanding business needs, and techniques for communicating the value of IT services. Although only 25 percent of Global 2000 IT organizations have organized groups to manage LOB relationships, 60 percent of them perform the function informally within existing management teams, with widely varying success. Analysts project that between 2003 and 2004, formal organizations will replace informal activities in 45 percent of companies, rising to 65 percent by 2006.

IT organizations must successfully integrate these functions by placing them within the same group. The most effective model places them within a COE, specifically inside the customer advocacy COE, which is where IT products are created, prices are managed, service levels are established, IT objectives and services are communicated to end users, and end-user satisfaction is measured and gauged. The IT organization is viewed as a value chain—a set of integrated services that meets customer requirements. Although the customer advocacy COE does not dictate performance requirements to other groups of the IT organization, it does have a role to influence project decisions, represent business needs, and ensure that the customer is always key in making IT investment decisions.

Simply put, the customer advocacy COE is the internal CRM group of IT. To demonstrate value, the IT organization first must understand its customers—their goals, mission statements, unique environments, and business requirements. Other processes included in this COE besides BRM are problem management, service request management, and service-level agreement management/service-level management. The binding theme that connects all these processes is the customer. As in CRM engagements, the customer advocacy COE is involved in the complete customer life cycle, including engagement, transaction, fulfillment, service delivery measurement, and improvement. Indeed, this COE acts as the customer voice to the IT organization. At the same time, it is the face shown by the IT organization to the customer.

IT Products and Pricing

A significant amount of fragmentation growth and overall disintermediation also occurs within the service provider market itself. Outsourcing is still growing close to 14 percent a year, and this is forcing IT organizations to take on the role of this internal service provider. Many organizations using this model end up with a broad IT product portfolio tied to the correct types of service levels and metrics and a particular price point. By 2003, more than 50 percent of IT organizations are expected to offer this type of structure.

An IT product is an encapsulation of IT services mapped to service levels at a published price for consumption. Several product, service-level, and pricing models can be applied. The net result of turning services into products enables "IT as a business" capabilities. Productization is important for all LOBs because it facilitates business-side predictability, specifically around costs. For IT organizations, it enables jobs, roles, and COEs to map out the work to be performed and the deliverables to be produced.

IT product catalogs are becoming a focal point for an expanded set of IT services, moving beyond end-user tools and application subscriptions to bundles of managed services offered to diverse constituencies. Flexibility and differentiation in product catalogs is expected to continue through 2005, delivered mainly via service-level customization and value-based product pricing. This trend is causing central IT groups to offer a new set of products:

- Managed infrastructure (such as server systems administration functions)

- Managed applications (such as application support and recovery management)

- Managed services (such as centralized procurement functions)

A survey of typical portfolios of IT products appears in Table 6.1.

Comprehensive IT product catalogs generally evolve to meet business-unit demands. As this happens, product catalog granularity will create administrative challenges, such as cost recovery, when a more diverse set of cost centers becomes a barrier to IT product definition. This is where the COE model (ultimately expanded throughout IT) facilitates the process. As this trend appears, IT groups increasingly will use sophisticated activity-based tracking and costing mechanisms and will need to become creative at splitting shared resources (the effect of service consolidation efforts).

Table 6.1 Typical IT Product Portfolio

Product Line	Product Examples	Product Pricing
Projects	ERP customization/ deployment	Priced per project
	In-house applications development	One-time charge
	Applications maintenance and enhancements	Fixed scope/price
	Infrastructure upgrade	Variable scope/price
Application Subscriptions	SAP R/3 subscription	Application/portfolio priced
	CRM subscription	One-time connect charge
	Financial application subscription	Monthly subscription
	Portfolio subscription	Usage charge-back
End-user Tools	Standard-managed desktop	Priced per seat
	Remote-managed desktop	Optional enhancements
	Power-managed desktop	Monthly allocation
	Telephone service	Service-level period
Shared Investments	Infrastructure upgrade	Allocation from overhead pool
	Strategic planning	May map to other products
	Disaster recovery	
Managed Infrastructure	Network (LAN/WAN) components	Monthly charges per bundle
	UNIX server management	Resource consumption
	Win2000/.NET server management	Direct pass-through
Managed Services	Procurement services	Time and materials
	Change management	Graduated price matrix
	Database administration	Percentage of external price
Managed Applications	Similar to subscription	Similar to subscription

Productizing Operations

All successful businesses must have a product model—a lesson that dot-com companies discovered during the "Internet bubble." No product model means no survival. Today's IT departments face a similar challenge. IT organizations need to identify who their customers are and what products and services those customers value. Failure to understand and provide value mean that the customers will look elsewhere for services.

Viewing IT organizations as providers of products means viewing their business model differently. Many IT organizations are run as a pure cost center or raw efficiency shop. An organization recognized only for reducing costs will face a perpetual struggle to gain additional resources. Although reducing costs is important, COE efforts are designed to show efficiency.

A series of steps can develop a plan of attack to create a product/pricing model, as shown in Figure 6.1. The first step is to identify and create a product model around the consumption constituency. What do the consumers (or customers) care about? What products and services, when bundled, make sense to them? The second is structuring service levels. Identify the services users understand and are willing to pay for, capture what the users feel are appropriate levels of service for the

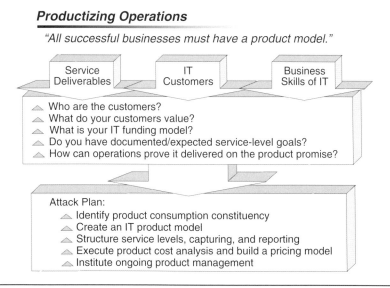

Figure 6.1 Steps in Productizing Operations

price, and report those levels back in the form of service-level agreements and performance reports. The way that IT organizations report performance and the metrics selected to prove performance are particularly important. Executing a product cost analysis to determine whether complex cost recovery charge-back methodology or pure allocation is an appropriate funding model is a good starting point. The idea is to communicate pricing efficiently with the end-user consumption constituency.

Product Models

Figure 6.2 shows an overall product model useful for IT organizations moving into this the direction of pricing and product models. Questions to ask in creating models include the following:

■ What products are being offered?

■ Who consumes these?

■ Who is seeing value in the particular product offerings?

A map can be laid out from the answers to these questions. It shows how the entire IT supply-and-delivery chain is constructed. Measurements of

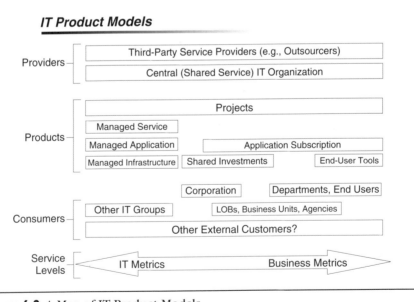

Figure 6.2 A Map of IT Product Models

the service products are mapped across the bottom of the figure. For some, IT metrics or IT-associated metrics such as those connected with a specific IT process are most appropriate. Service-level-related measurements are more business-oriented and communicate value more clearly to the business user.

Pricing Models

This approach is not an appropriate strategy for all IT organizations. The predominant driver as to whether an IT group goes after building a complex, robust IT product model is its funding strategy. If an IT organization is funded merely as a corporate subsidy itself, it does not have to track or report IT resource allocation or perform true cost recovery. Such an IT group does not have a strong incentive to build this model to end up being a real service provider with a real product model. That IT group also has a much harder time proving value to the organization versus the IT group trying to package what it does and performing true cost recovery from the business side, mapped to consumption of real IT products and services.

Increasingly, due to financial reasons, hardware and software resource ownership is found in business units or LOB IT groups, while the support for such resources may rest with a central IT group. In such cases, a particular resource, such as a server or printer, may have to be quoted at a particular support cost to be paid by the business user. These arrangements break the typical bundled IT offerings found in initial product models.

Therefore, central shared services groups are exposing high degrees of granularity in their internal costs. One mistake that often is made in pricing these offerings is tying the price points to a specific infrastructure combination—for example, Oracle 9 on Windows 2000/.NET on a Hewlett-Packard server. Research shows that such pricing influences undesirable buying behavior as "buyers" try to second-guess the pricing and go with the "cheapest" model rather than the most appropriate "fit." In this example, because Oracle support is less expensive on Windows 2000 versus UNIX, the user may select Windows 2000/.NET rather than choose the operating system best suited to the application. To avoid this issue, IT organizations should indicate pricing models that take into consideration the enterprise architecture requirements to realize long-term benefits.

Also, to further mitigate this buying behavior, IT organizations building these offerings into their product catalogs must focus on two dimensions—an abstraction complexity and particular service level—and build these into a product pricing matrix. The complexity and service-level intersection point must reflect total internal support costs. For most items, a minimum of three and a maximum of seven complexity levels should be defined, as shown in Figure 6.3, while three service levels should be used. Complexity level is determined primarily by the degree of standardization, scale, locality, and heterogeneity. When a buyer selects a managed offering, the selection then would fit into the pricing matrix appropriately. Accommodations must be made for buyer demands that may fall outside the matrix, and a pricing assessment and oversight function would be triggered

Research shows a positive response from users to this type of price model, but it also can cause additional and unforeseen demands that must be handled. For example, organizations that have begun charging back managed network services directly based on network bandwidth consumption then are approached by their business users to help optimize their network usage and "get the cost down." IT organizations moving to a managed product model must anticipate and be ready to respond to such requests to ensure overall client satisfaction.

Some IT organizations will get requests from users to unbundle a product to select specific elements from an overall package. An uplift charge (10 to 30 percent) built into the pricing model for unbundling,

Service Levels / Complexity	Basic	Standard	Premium
Extreme	$$$	$$$+	$$$$
High	$$+	$$$	$$$+
Normal	$$	$$+	$$$
Low	$+	$$	$$+
Commodity	$	$+	$$

Figure 6.3 Cost Matrix Comparing Service Levels and Complexity

covers the cost of customizing and supporting a nonhomogeneous product model.

Another hindrance to the pricing model is when it includes any offerings based on pure measurement (such as resource consumption and user accounting). Often, these types of measurement capture for charge-back or cost recovery must be custom built and can be expensive to initiate and maintain. IT groups must understand the inherent overhead costs in administering any cost-recovery model. Higher aggregation of service elements under a product—and avoidance of a restrictive à la carte model—leads to costly tracking and billing administrative overhead. For shared services IT groups, the problem of accurate service pricing will get more difficult as server size grows and multiple user cost centers have to share single infrastructure element or application cost. The managed service offering, typically focused on execution of an IT process and predominantly consisting of labor costs, can be charged on a fixed basis or a time-and-materials (T&M) model, or on a piecework structure that takes into account the amount per change handled and the percentage per procurement contract.

Organizations undertaking their first-generation efforts around productizing should think about those critical products most exposed to their customer base, such as desktop support. Begin with a service description that describes the scope. Questions to ask are these: What is included? What is not included? What kind of computing environment is it? What service levels are expected? What kind of contract terms do we have?

IT products and their metrics are exposed or delivered as the value currency. Failure to collect those metrics (which show the value back to the business) invalidates the purpose of product catalog creation.

Cost Variability

Distributed applications are challenging the traditional way to do cost recovery. In the mainframe space, resource utilization charge-back was typically based on MIPS, storage, or output consumption. Those models do not always fit in many types of modern applications. A tremendous lack of standard user-level accounting data exists across all technologies. The absence of this data is a barrier to some newer cost-recovery models.

Pricing is influenced or driven by the costs that support the particular services provided. For example, if the user population is centralized, the cost figures or implications will be lower. A more dispersed or remote environment tends to raise the cost levels. Similarly, flexible service-level requirements tend to lower costs. The more stringent service levels become and the more specific products and services provided around service levels become, the more influential they are as cost drivers. To an extent, improving productivity can enhance service levels; beyond that, improved service levels are linked to increased investment because they lead to increased costs. Figure 6.4 shows some drivers of cost variability.

Other cost drivers include the extent of applications and infrastructure standardization. Increased standardization leverages existing skill sets, driving costs down. A heterogeneous environment with a wide array of technologies to be supported increases support costs. This notion of "adaptive infrastructure" as a means of reducing complexity is outlined in the book *The Adaptive Enterprise: IT Infrastructure Strategies to Manage Change and Enable Growth*, published in this series.

Enterprise management can reduce investment decision risks because a formal method of strategic planning/architecting can be institutionalized and refined to enable considerable time-savings. The higher

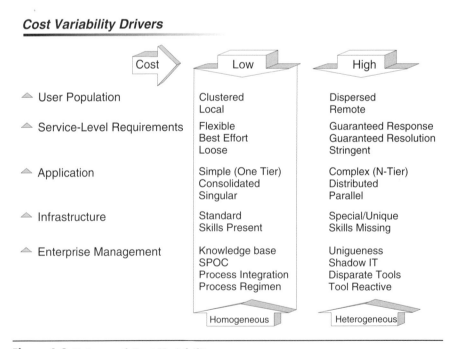

Cost Variability Drivers

	Cost	Low	High
User Population		Clustered Local	Dispersed Remote
Service-Level Requirements		Flexible Best Effort Loose	Guaranteed Response Guaranteed Resolution Stringent
Application		Simple (One Tier) Consolidated Singular	Complex (N-Tier) Distributed Parallel
Infrastructure		Standard Skills Present	Special/Unique Skills Missing
Enterprise Management		Knowledge base SPOC Process Integration Process Regimen	Uniqueness Shadow IT Disparate Tools Tool Reactive
		Homogeneous	Heterogeneous

Figure 6.4 Drivers of Cost Variability

the levels of integration and discipline achieved via enterprise management, the more cost levels can be driven down.

Cost—Allocation—Price Strategies

As IT becomes more closely related to the business, organizations are migrating to newer accounting charge-back models in an attempt to tie the actual IT value back to the business in more real and direct terms. Figure 6.5 portrays a mechanism to help map pricing back to allocation strategy. Performing the actual cost mechanism begins with identifying the cost pools. After you have identified and added the various costs associated to the different cost pools, you influence them or modify them by the different decision drivers.

The four commandments of product/pricing strategy are:

■ The cost/pricing mechanism must be understandable to all "buying" constituencies.

■ Cost/price must be predictable (on the buy side) for business-planning purposes.

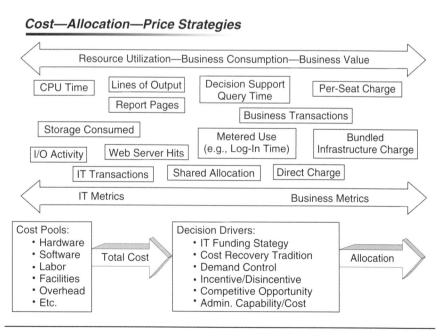

Cost—Allocation—Price Strategies

Figure 6.5 Cost—Allocation—Price Strategies

- Cost/price must be clearly related to IT value received (actual or perceived).

- IT organization supplied services must be priced competitively with competing open-market services.

IT organizations should determine the unit price for desktop, project, and application subscription services, and compare the internal cost with outsourcing prices. This process should be undertaken in a formal benchmark, whereby service levels are tightly coupled to competitive market prices and cost overheads in managing outsourced arrangements are considered. If the internal cost is too high and cannot be driven down to match outsourcing prices, the assessed service should be outsourced. Otherwise, IT operations groups should confidently position this service to business units as matching commercial standards. This will raise business units' understanding of IT services and increase their trust in the in-house service quality and cost-efficiency.

The road map to establishing a charge-back strategy is as follows:

1. Calculate the service costs.

2. Benchmarks.

3. Make outsourcing decisions.

To determine the service cost, each budget element should be analyzed and apportioned to deduce the total cost of every application server and all related infrastructure needed to support it (such as storage and network usage). Servers should include mainframe, UNIX, Windows 2000/ .NET server, and LAN. The desktop service cost should include PCs, palmtops, laptops, and LAN servers. The application subscription service cost should include the data center, technical support, and WAN.

Some budget elements are easy to allocate to servers, and others are difficult. In this light, assumptions should be made to distribute cost—for example, taking a direct pass-through charge-back approach that distributes cost to individual departments or business units that are using the application on the server. Additional desires must be considered, such as building in costs for infrastructure or using pricing strategies to influence buying behavior. Subsequently, IT operations groups should aggregate the various servers' cost to deduce service cost. The allocation mechanism, or cost per user/employee/department, must then be set. After this is implemented, the tracking, billing detail, and reporting should happen. A yearly period-variance adjustment must occur to handle over/undercharges.

Product Catalog

The great majority of product catalogs today are first-generation efforts. They attempt to define the function and scope of IT services in non-technical terms. Budgets remain fixed corporate allocations (rather than charge-back), and product catalogs serve to define and explain services rather than to set the scope and price. Although such product catalogs help users understand the IT services provided, they do little toward the ultimate objective of making IT expenditures part of the business decision-making process.

Second-generation product catalogs require support and involvement by the senior levels of company management. To properly structure products, the IT organization must undergo fundamental changes in four areas, as shown in Figure 6.6.

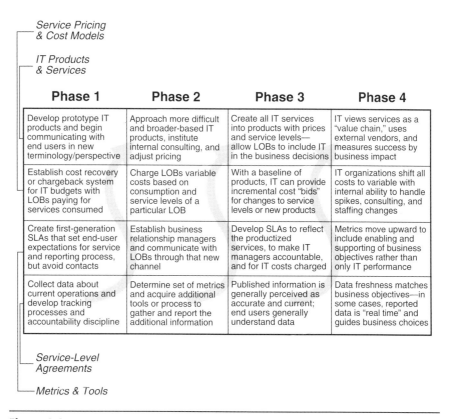

	Phase 1	Phase 2	Phase 3	Phase 4
Service Pricing & Cost Models / *IT Products & Services*	Develop prototype IT products and begin communicating with end users in new terminology/perspective	Approach more difficult and broader-based IT products, institute internal consulting, and adjust pricing	Create all IT services into products with prices and service levels—allow LOBs to include IT in the business decisions	IT views services as a "value chain," uses external vendors, and measures success by business impact
	Establish cost recovery or chargeback system for IT budgets with LOBs paying for services consumed	Charge LOBs variable costs based on consumption and service levels of a particular LOB	With a baseline of products, IT can provide incremental cost "bids" for changes to service levels or new products	IT organizations shift all costs to variable with internal ability to handle spikes, consulting, and staffing changes
	Create first-generation SLAs that set end-user expectations for service and reporting process, but avoid contacts	Establish business relationship managers and communicate with LOBs through that new channel	Develop SLAs to reflect the productized services, to make IT managers accountable, and for IT costs charged	Metrics move upward to include enabling and supporting of business objectives rather than only IT performance
Service-Level Agreements / *Metrics & Tools*	Collect data about current operations and develop tracking processes and accountability discipline	Determine set of metrics and acquire additional tools or process to gather and report the additional information	Published information is generally perceived as accurate and current; end users generally understand data	Data freshness matches business objectives—in some cases, reported data is "real time" and guides business choices

Figure 6.6 The IT Service Value Chain

Funding must shift from fixed corporate allocations to a charge-back methodology based on the services consumed. This change is deployed most effectively with a phased rollout (most companies start with desktop services) that enables business units to understand IT services and consider IT expenses in the context of business investment decisions.

Infrastructure decisions must be made by a panel of IT executives and business leaders working jointly to assess and invest in common company-wide capabilities on which all other technology investments depend, for example, network bandwidth.

Service levels must be established around the products to set end-user expectations for technical services and problem-resolution support. To establish service levels and corresponding pricing, the specific scope must be carefully defined and articulated (similar to outsourcing agreements, but without the contractual formality). Incremental services and service levels require higher prices that are passed along to the users. This cultural change alone often requires several years of phased change.

Accountability and user support must pervade the behavior and decision making of all IT employees. The IT organization must have tools and processes to measure and report on service levels effectively. Many analysts predict that by 2005, most IT managers will be compensated largely according to performance against service-level objectives.

After the product catalog is established and users have adapted to the above changes, the IT organization will face increasing pressure to justify its quality and price of services to those of external service providers. It is critical that IT products be structured similar to those of outsourcing companies so that accurate benchmarking can be performed. IT organizations usually learn significant lessons about effective and efficient IT operations during this process—and outsource select components of IT operations where improvements are available.

Although the specific structures of product catalogs vary widely, nearly every Global 2000 IT organization uses models that divide IT services into end-user tools, application services, and projects (including internal consulting):

■ *End-user tools* include computers, telephones, pagers, and other communication devices. Desktop applications, e-mail, and Internet access are usually bundled into this package. This service is usually the first that IT organizations develop into a product because the services are clearly discernable by users and the costs are better defined. Prices for end-user tools are specified as "per device per month" and should include a menu of choices (with varying costs), for laptops, engineering and graphics workstations, and so forth, that are required throughout the corporation. Service levels should include metrics for procurement, install, move, add, and change functions, and for problem resolution.

■ *Application services.* Global 2000 IT organizations have hundreds of applications to support. The model for pricing and supporting applications depends on the degree of centralization across the corporation. Business units that already own application development/maintenance should be charged only for hosting expenses, and corporations with centralized application development and maintenance may charge back for all services. All corporations have enterprise applications provided centrally. Such applications should be charged on a "per user per month" basis. Some companies vary pricing by level of users. Service levels should include application availability and response time, which will require new tools for most IT operations.

■ *Projects* are the most easily priced because they usually are aligned or enable incremental business activity. Global 2000 IT organizations are introducing the concept of an internal consulting organization. Business units may contract for projects or simply additional headcount to work on a specific issue or project. Internal consulting becomes completely dysfunctional in IT organizations without direct charge-back capabilities.

Development of a robust IT product model is an initial milestone in operating like a business. The IT product catalog embodies the IT services that are provided, along with initial service-level expectations and cost.

Marketing the Value of IT

The most common pitfall that advanced IT operations groups encounter is the inability to communicate and demonstrate value in business terms. Because perceived value often may have more weight than real value, IT organizations consistently and constantly must focus on communications as a means to positively affect perceptions.

Marketing the IT organization increases the perception that IT adds value to the business, raising the enterprise's recognition of its dependence on the IT organization and helping to ensure that the CIO is (and is perceived to be) a business partner. CIOs should actively promote their IT organization to ensure that that their enterprise obtains the maximum business value from its product and thus to move up the perceived value chain toward full partnership with LOBs in driving the business.

Research indicates that one of the major challenges IT organizations face today is creating the perception of delivering value to the business. Because business exists more and more as a function of data, IT organizations need to sell to their business colleagues the fact that IT can and should be leveraged for business value and growth. Analysts project that by 2003, more than 50 percent of the Global 2000 will have a formal marketing arm in their IT organizations, ensuring that the business understands the full value information has to the bottom line. Marketing has become one of the four core IT functions, along with planning, integration, and maintenance. The marketing function has three major elements: capabilities and product catalog, relationship management, and promotion.

Business Relationship Management

Currently, more than 60 percent of enterprise IT organizations have individuals focused on account management. Because of this, IT groups are likely to evolve from the current account manager role to BRM positions. The *relationship manager*'s (RM) primary role is the liaison between the customer and the IT organization. The RM communicates opportunities, enablement, and value outwardly. In addition, he acts as a funnel and facilitator of requirements, issues, and concerns inwardly. Consequently, RMs must have complete familiarity with their customers' goals and business objectives to present a tailored value proposition in terms that are meaningful to the customer. The most successful RMs have spent significant time working in the business unit but now report into the IT organization. Previous work in the business unit gives the RM the background required for the job. Reporting into the IT organization ensures that the RM is not perceived as the "enforcer" to beat up the IT organization.

IT organizations must establish formal job requirements for managing the relationships with business units. BRM will not succeed if it is merely added on to the responsibilities of overworked IT managers.

An RM usually spends the first few months listening to the complaints and problems about the IT organization. RMs become a primary channel for communicating (and marketing) the value and performance of the IT organization in addition to helping IT understand business requirements better. RMs individually and BRM generally must be part of a broader, integrated communication plan managed across the IT organization, including customer satisfaction reports, service-level reports, and other marketing activities.

The primary objective of the BRM organization and the activities of BRM account managers change over time. BRM can be categorized into three phases, each with varying priorities.

■ *Phase 1—Inbound:* Typical activities during the first phase focus on building relationships with business executives and beginning to function as an account manager/customer representative. BRM account managers perform little in problem resolution but should become established as the primary contact for the LOB. Approximately 30 percent of BRM organizations also are involved in a team effort to create and implement SLAs.

■ *Phase 2—Outbound:* As relationships become established and glaring problems are resolved, BRM shifts toward "outbound" activities of setting expectations, increasing clarity of IT capabilities/deliverables, creating product/service catalogs, and reporting on SLA performance. During this phase, BRM begins interacting with technical and project teams to improve the alignment of IT services with business needs. Account managers help position, sell, and communicate the services, methodologies, and operations of IT operations to the LOBs.

■ *Phase 3—Enable:* As an enabling organization, BRM becomes a pivotal role in both business and IT strategy. Within the LOB, account managers sit on teams for new business products/offerings and represent IT capability, support, and innovation. Within the IT organization, account managers work as pivotal members with the project management office. Successful BRM account managers aid the business by having the IT organization included in business strategy meetings and by representing LOB interests in key planning and strategy sessions for IT operations.

As the IT organization develops product catalogs and SLAs, the RM plays a role in helping LOBs understand offerings and expected performance levels. RMs become the communication arm that represents the IT organization outward to the user constituency. Throughout the phases of IT service chain evolution, RMs communicate problems, changes, and opportunities with LOBs. Moreover, RMs understand LOB business models, objectives, and ongoing changes and can be the IT representative who guides (at a high level) IT strategy supporting the business constituency. RMs should sit on the executive staff of the LOB but must report into the IT organization, necessitating senior-level, intelligent professionals with technical prowess and business sense.

With established product catalogs, service levels, and IT cost recovery structures, RMs rapidly and responsibly can provide cost estimates for both long- and short-term business projects, enabling IT expenditures to become a part of the business decision process. As IT organizations become increasingly responsive and establish internal consulting organizations, RMs can help LOBs learn to understand and leverage internal resources rather than turn to external consulting or outsourcing organizations—further reducing project costs and increasing the "reputation" of the internal IT organization.

For most companies, business liaison roles exist within multiple parts of the IT organization (frequently, applications groups and operations), but most are ineffective in the context of rigorous business relationship management. Moreover, relationship management groups exist in many companies to manage outsourcing relationships. To provide the business customer with an end-to-end view of IT services and support, these roles are likely to converge as part of a customer-advocacy COE.

Value/Metric Reporting

Once established, RMs (and likewise IT executives) want metrics that indicate the success of BRM activities. Early metrics are closely related to overall IT operational performance, such as customer satisfaction. IT organizations lacking metrics that measure end-user satisfaction are equally deficient in quantifiable metrics specific to BRM. First-generation metrics often include the following checklists:

- Design the categorization scheme of end users, LOBs, and other constituencies to be consistent, if not integrated, with problem management processes. RMs should not displace problem management processes or help-desk organizations.

- Determine key priorities and methods by which LOBs determine and assess IT organization performance. RMs must be careful to avoid being defensive during this discovery exercise.

- Begin measuring and surveying LOBs for satisfaction with the IT organization overall and for methods of communication specifically. A statistical baseline must be developed by which improvements and changes can be monitored.

■ Develop a reporting and communications methodology to report timelines, establish expectations, remind about successes, and warn of pending problems. LOB managers often fail to recognize that an element of risk is associated with any project and that cutting-edge technology is not automatic.

Developing sophisticated IT measures enhances the ability to validate BRM with specific metrics. Although the BRM team is involved in collecting and assessing overall IT metrics, it must also focus on measuring the efficacy and efficiency of the BRM organization as follows:

■ Savings from effective IT-LOB relationships. Although this metric is always an estimate, RMs frequently track project modifications, cancellations, or other significant changes. If IT managers place too much emphasis on this metric, the numbers become exaggerated and the value diminished.

■ Percentage of service-level agreements against internal targets that are developed and regularly reported to LOBs.

■ Percentage of application development and maintenance budget spent on project definition and management against internal improvement targets.

■ Number of IT-LOB relationship problems that are facilitated or mediated by the BRM organization. RMs should route routine end-user support through the help desk.

■ Customer satisfaction results from LOB "customers" specific to the support, effort, and quality of the BRM team.

Enabling BRM emphasizes business impact/results and attempts to correlate IT investments and priorities with business objectives. It requires a level of trust between IT and LOBs, which extends to mutual interdependency rather than mutual blame and finger pointing. Customer satisfaction is routinely measured via numerous channels, including the help desk and user surveys.

Market analysts predict that customer satisfaction will constitute 15 to 25 percent of performance objectives for IT managers by 2006. IT metrics will include the impact of IT on business activities, including efficiency improvements, cost reductions, and customer relationship improvements. The BRM team will lead or participate in IT marketing initiatives, including service-level reporting and creation of IT annual reports.

The IT Annual Report

Most companies report on their business performance via an annual report (along with quarterly updates) that shows how well they are doing financially and how well their various business initiatives are performing. This concept was first introduced in Chapter 5. An increasing number of IT groups are taking advantage of the same kind of communication mechanisms. Frequently, these groups create an annual report that discusses what they are working on and then market the report to different internal and external customer audiences, including LOBs, internal IT groups, and business leaders. This report can be supplemented by abridged versions published on a quarterly basis. Additionally, to complete the analogy to a business performance report, a mechanism should exist for IT to make specific announcements on an interim basis. Much of what is driving this is the idea that IT should not only be setting proper expectations, but also be reiterating those expectations in relation to performance.

Topics in an IT annual report might be covered in the following order:

1. Introduction/letter from senior management
2. Client success stories
3. Status of major projects
4. Where do the projects stand versus the plan?
5. How do actual budgets compare to projections?
6. Business value that IT brings to the organization
7. Metrics
8. Internal versus external customers
9. Efficiency
10. Effectiveness
11. Capability
12. Financial reports/budgets
13. List of major future initiatives and their business value

A business annual report typically starts with a series of success stories and quotes from satisfied customers. The IT annual report should ask, "Which business customers funded the major IT projects, and were these projects successful?" The IT organization should find out how customers feel about completed projects and what value was gained from them, and then work this information into the report in the form of success stories and "happy customer" quotes.

Another section in a typical corporate annual report covers financials. IT needs to report matters such as whether projects were on budget and what the ongoing operating costs were. The IT group's equivalent to corporate financials would be information such as overall IT expenditures as a percentage of the company's revenue or earnings. Unit-cost information and analysis would be included in this section of the IT annual report as well. An important issue discussed in Chapter 5 was how to align the organization's business goals with the appropriate IT metrics. Some IT groups may choose to incorporate the goal/metric snapshots from their PMM in their IT annual reports to better show business/IT alignment.

In a separate section, the report should discuss key future initiatives that IT plans on undertaking, such as interesting new technologies and how those technologies might be applied to major upcoming projects. It is important to include references as to how this will help the business. Another item in this section might be a chart showing unit-cost futures and how they will be trending downward, even though overall budgets will likely still rise due to increasing demand and needed capacity. Such expectations must be properly set.

Three other sections belong in the IT annual report: staffing, customer satisfaction, and time to market. Corporate annual reports usually mention how many people the business employs. The IT department's report should talk about how many employees and contractors are on staff as a percentage of the company's total head count or as a percentage of various LOB employees. A page or two should be devoted to metrics on customer satisfaction; this information can be pulled directly from help-desk and trouble-ticketing systems. Examples of items included might be overall customer satisfaction, top 10 customer issues, mean time to resolution, and other relevant customer satisfaction issues or metrics. One of the newer metrics included in corporate annual reports is time to market. IT needs to include this as well, showing the value it has provided by getting its own products to market faster.

Simply creating the IT annual report is not enough. In fact, it is just the beginning. The annual report must be communicated to the audiences that need to see it. Putting it on the company intranet and then e-mailing a hyperlink to everyone on the business side of the company is a fine idea. However, the board members, high-level executives (CEO or CFO), and managers running certain LOBs that need to see certain sections of the report should be targeted in a different way: The IT organization should send them the excerpts of most interest to them, along with the same hyperlink back to the full report. For very senior business executives, setting up a brief meeting between them and the CIO (or other top IT executives) and going through the IT annual report with them is recommended. They should be asked what they prefer to see and whether the information that matters most to them is included. This gets the business executives involved in the process so that the IT organization knows what they want to see. Future buy-in will be greatly enhanced when IT reports are presented in this way.

The RM is the best person for authoring the annual report. The RM administers SLAs, represents the key contact for business, and often is hired from the business side.

Other Marketing Techniques

Promoting the IT organization entails a true public relations (PR) effort. As part of this effort, IT organizations should focus on creating a marketing plan and defining and communicating a clear vision, mission, and principles of the IT organization, including the crafting of a compelling value statement that all members of the IT organization know, understand, and can communicate.

PR Campaign. CIOs should proactively undertake a PR campaign that answers two fundamental user question: (1) What has the IT team done for me lately? (2) What does the IT department plan to do for me tomorrow? The key elements of the PR campaign help CIOs communicate IT organizational alignment with the following business imperatives:

- Improving competitiveness
- Streamlining processes
- Improving customer service
- Meeting regulatory requirements
- Reducing costs and increasing profitability
- Improving flexibility (adaptability) and implementing changes quickly (agility)
- Enabling more accurate assessment and forecasting of technology costs and benefits
- Guiding internal technology decisions (and, in some cases, business investment decisions)

Five Marketing Activities. CIOs should adopt a simple, five-point marketing plan and an ongoing PR promotion campaign that answers perceived questions from the CEO, management committee members, and LOB executives, such as these:

- How will the IT group help me meet my performance objectives?
- What will the IT staff do to improve customer service levels?
- How can the IT department leverage and deploy emerging technology to improve my business?
- Why is this technology platform/program/service costing so much and taking so long to implement?

The five points of the marketing plan are:

1. Performing a baseline assessment: What business is the IT organization in? Determine the IT organization's current position with a focus on vision, mission, business model, and technology architecture. A vision and mission statement should be defined and communicated. This helps CIOs communicate to LOB colleagues exactly what services the IT organization performs.

2. Building a "value" case and communicating the value message: What strengths does the IT organization have that people know (or should know) about? Every organization has strengths, and the people with whom it conducts business ultimately judge the IT organization. If LOB colleagues were asked to list IT organizational strengths, how would they respond? CIOs should articulate and communicate the IT organization's value message. Does the IT organization acknowledge how much money is spent and the value of the goods and services provided?

3. Communicating sourcing strategy: What weaknesses does the IT organization have that people know (or should know) about? All organizations have weaknesses. Like strengths, they can be used to judge the IT organization's value. In the minds of the IT organization's clients and executive management, what are the IT organization's weaknesses and commoditized services? Does the IT organization have a plan to selectively outsource non-core competencies and commoditized, low-value-add services? Has the IT organization defined and communicated its sourcing strategy and firmly established its role as the general contractor?

4. Viewing threats as potential opportunities to create and communicate value: What are the opportunities and threats that relate to the business? Opportunities and threats are factors that CIOs think they cannot control. For example, new government regulations may require special reporting and compliance standards (as well as wholesale system changes, new applications, or staff education and training). This may be an opportunity for the IT organization to tackle the threat head-on and assume a leadership position, fill the need, and demonstrate value to LOB executives and senior management.

5. Focusing on the products and services that produce the greatest benefits: What does the IT organization have that is both marketable and, more importantly, perceived as having the greatest value? CIOs should focus on the products and services that produce the greatest benefit for the enterprise. Pareto's Principle states that 20 percent of the products or services sold produce 80 percent of the revenue. Therefore, CIOs should actively focus on those as portfolio applications and market them as high-value-added services.

Conclusion

This book has explained how to move a company's IT operations from current levels to the mark of excellence known as best practices. It has explained the planning and analysis required to make this step forward and the transformation of IT operations into processes and then into COEs. This last step serves to raise operations to a new role in which it is the product that the IT department sells to the rest of the enterprise.

For the modern IT department to be successful with this model, it must concentrate on what will be a fairly new discipline: marketing its products and its value to the enterprise—just like any LOB. The degree to which it is successful in this endeavor determines the funding and fate that the IT organization can expect to enjoy in the years ahead.

Chapter **7**

Process Catalog

T he Process Catalog is an IT organization's single source for the definition of IT operations processes. The Process Catalog is invaluable
in the management and continuous improvement of these processes.

How to Use This Catalog

Readers should mold this Process Catalog to meet the needs of their IT
organizations. We have included 38 sample processes in this chapter.
The number of processes that an organization would include in its own
catalog, as well as detail in which they are described, depends on the
extent of the OE effort. Readers are encouraged to delete, rename,
expand, or collapse the processes that require modification in their analysis.

At a minimum, each process should be measured according to automation and stability levels. Processes are a balance of manual and automated
tasks. Stable or "commoditized" processes introduce opportunities for
automation. Target values represent the automation or stability levels as
implemented in best-practice organizations. Such values are subjective,
but provide a baseline from which to begin gap analysis and process
improvement.

A generic explanation of the Process Catalog entries is provided as a
preface to the alphabetically ordered catalog entries.

125

Form and Content of Process Catalog Entries

Each Process Catalog entry has the form shown on these two pages. The entry begins with a definition of the IT business process.

Below this description you will find a scale indicating the current automation and stability levels of a process. You can highlight the numbers that represents the current level of automation and stability for each process at your site. Shading indicates typical values for best-practices organizations.

Items in the catalog use two styles of bullet. Solid bullets (■) serve only to mark the item. Open bullets (❐) indicate items that you should compare to your site's current processes. You can mark the items that you have implemented.

1 2 3 4 5 6 7 8 9 10	1 2 3 4 5 6 7 8 9 10
Manual Automatic	Dynamic Stable

Tasks

Tasks are the activities that typically make up the process as it is implemented at many large firms today.

■ Not all tasks are listed—only those viewed as especially important or easily overlooked

■ You should add tasks unique to your IT organization

Skills

Skills itemizes the typically required skills and abilities to implement this process.

■ Not all skills are listed—only those viewed as especially important or easily overlooked

Staffing

Staffing indicates typical staffing in large IT organizations.

❐ At smaller sites, one employee might perform the functions of several staff members

❐ For sites pursuing best practices, all positions mentioned in this section should have counterparts in current staff responsibilities

Automation Technology

Automation Technology is a list of representative technologies that can automate the tasks that make up the IT process.

❐ Inclusion in the list does not constitute an endorsement

❐ Nor is absence from the list a tacit comment

Best Practices

Best Practices are the activities that the best-run IT organizations use.

❑ Best-practice items should be compared to activities at your site as part of the gap analysis

Metrics

Metrics are the quantifiable aspects of operations that should be tracked for purposes of measuring quality of deliverables and success or failure of the implementation of best practices.

❑ Metrics are commonly compared year after year

❑ Metrics can sometimes be compared to external benchmarks

Process Integration

Process Integration refers to other IT processes in this Catalog that integrate with the current process.

■ This information is useful when making changes in the current process as it indicates other processes that might be affected

Futures

Futures indicates any likely advances in technology that could affect the way that this process is performed at IT sites.

■ Futures may also include changes in the manner in which business is conducted, for example, a shift to e-Business transactions

Application Optimization

This process seeks to enhance application efficiency and performance while minimizing cost. For new applications, it seeks enforcement of the tenets of the production-acceptance process and assurance that customer service expectations are met in these areas: operational procedures, run-time improvement, connectivity and middleware optimization, and tuning of internal logic.

Automation	Stability
1 2 3 4 5 6 7 8 9 10 Manual Automatic	1 2 3 4 5 6 7 8 9 10 Dynamic Stable

Tasks	Skills
■ Train entry-level personnel	■ Expertise in using various application-tuning tools
■ Define standards for applications	
■ Tune job control language and programs	■ Expert knowledge of JCL, scripts, processes and their optimization
■ Write recommendations to application owners	■ Familiarity with the performance characteristics of storage media
■ Ensure compliance with production acceptance processes	■ Working knowledge of change, ADLC and SCM processes, common programming languages (Cobol, C, C++, Fortran, and Java) and environments, e.g., Visual Studio.NET
	■ Good communications skills
	■ Working knowledge of business processes and application flow

Staffing	Automation Technology
❏ Quality control specialist	❏ Tuning tools (such as Strobe, TSA/PPE, Architeck)
❏ Production coordinator	
❏ Tuning specialist	❏ JCL generation and optimization tools

Best Practices	**Metrics**
❐ Consistent, cross-platform approach to application optimization ❐ Periodic review of new technology impacts on business applications ❐ Regular reassessment of technology needs over time to assure that (1) old hardware and software are performing adequately and (2) new technology may provide a stepwise improvement in performance ❐ Continuous application performance improvement ❐ Explicit definitions of critical requirements for new and enhanced applications	❐ Percentage improvement in tuned applications ❐ Number of errors in changed applications ❐ Amount of investment relative to degree of improvement ❐ System resources consumed ❐ Number of emergency optimization needs/requests ❐ Average time to respond to new requests ❐ Number of tuning efforts/analyst

Process Integration	**Futures**
■ No Items	■ Automated tuning and self-optimizing applications ■ Application componentization and reuse

Asset Management

This process aims to manage and optimize the cost, retention, and ultimate disposal of IT assets including hardware, software, and communications infrastructure.

Automation	Stability
1 2 3 **4** 5 6 7 8 9 10 Manual　　　　　　　Automatic	1 2 3 4 5 6 **7** 8 9 10 Dynamic　　　　　　　Stable

Tasks	Skills
■ Maintain and manage the acquisition, maintenance (costs) and disposal of all IT assets ■ Manage vendor contracts and associated terms and conditions ■ Manage portfolios based on optimal "refresh cycles" ■ Track actual versus projected for IT equipment and staff	■ Basic knowledge of accounting principles ■ Ability to define processes and procedures for acquisition/disposal ■ Ability to develop approaches to simplify customer involvement

Staffing	Automation Technology
❏ Asset management specialist ❏ Customer liaison ❏ Financial analyst	❏ CA-MICS, IBM SLR, Merrill Consultants' MXG

Best Practices

❏ Integrated process and automation for managing IT assets

❏ Integration of asset management with corporate processes/automation

❏ Use of defined standards for asset life, disposal, and so forth

❏ Efficient corporate process for ordering/acquisition

Metrics

❏ Number of products/number of staff

❏ Budget/number of staff

❏ Savings (by category)/year

Process Integration

■ Inventory management

■ Configuration management

■ Asset tracking

Futures

■ Seamless integration with corporate tools/processes

■ Higher reporting relationship (directly to CIO)

■ More direct tie-in to Customer Advocacy COE (including BRM)

■ Participation in go/no-go buying scenarios

Budget Management

In addition to tracking costs versus budgets and reporting variances, this process aims to manage and reconcile incurred costs with cost recovery, plus provide out-year estimates and modeling for new budgets.

Automation	Stability
1 2 **3** 4 5 6 7 8 9 10	1 2 3 4 5 6 **7** 8 9 10
Manual Automatic	Dynamic Stable

Tasks	Skills
■ Maintain budget, actual versus planned	■ Detailed understanding of full IT inventory and related processes
■ Define and enforce processes for budget compliance	■ Basic financial/budgeting skills
■ Enforce spending limits based on policies/standards	■ Cost accounting knowledge
	■ Familiarity with technology metrics and trends
	■ Understanding of corporate budget process/rules

Staffing	Automation Technology
❐ Budget specialist	❐ Financial systems for budget planning
❐ Accountant	❐ Cost accounting systems
❐ Financial analyst	❐ Forecasting systems

Best Practices	Metrics
❐ Use of automated systems that track actual and budgeted monies ❐ Semi-annual budget iterations	❐ Actual versus planned costs ❐ Group costs/budget value ❐ Quantity of resources/cost

Process Integration	Futures
■ No Items	■ Automated system to tract budgets and actual costs ■ Linkage with forecast systems ■ Automatic budget planning based on forecast ■ "What if" modeling for various technology business alternatives

Business Continuity

This process aims to provide continuous availability or contingent business processes as required in emergencies and extraordinary events. It develops business-continuity strategies and tactics (disaster recovery), identifies document recovery requirements for critical business applications, and also manages backup and archival processes for critical data.

Automation	Stability
1 2 3 **4** 5 6 7 8 9 10 Manual Automatic	1 2 3 4 5 6 **7** 8 9 10 Dynamic Stable

Tasks	Skills
■ Prepare and maintain a business continuity plan (BCP) ■ Communicate with suppliers and customers regarding disaster-recovery requirements ■ Arrange and coordinate with hot-site, e-vault providers ■ Integrate BCP with production acceptance processes ■ Define standards around business continuity for customers	■ Expertise in scenario planning ■ Knowledge of technologies critical to information recovery

Staffing	Automation Technology
❏ Disaster-recovery specialist ❏ Project manager ❏ Business/IT liaison	❏ Disaster-recovery management software (Sunrise, Arise) ❏ Disaster-recovery planning software (PC-based)

Best Practices	Metrics
❏ Common continuity plans for the enterprise ❏ Update plan twice a year ❏ Test plan three times per year, with one actual, one simulated, and one unplanned test ❏ BCP has equal emphasis on business recovery and technology recovery ❏ Optimize use of third-party disaster-recovery facilities ❏ Integrate disaster recovery requirements with production acceptance process ❏ Ability to perform integrated testing/recovery across IT platforms	❏ A mean time to recovery (in relation to pattern) ❏ Cost per business segment, per volume of technology protected ❏ Stratified cost structure by pattern for systems and application with availability requirements as follows: instantaneous, within 24 hours, 24–72 hours, 5–7 days ❏ Cost /MB of archived data
Process Integration	**Futures**
■ Disk storage management ■ Tape management	■ Disaster recovery built into tape/storage subsystems, packaged applications ■ Better cross-platform software for disaster recovery ■ Improved simulation (scripting) software to minimize the need for business area involvement in disaster-recovery testing ■ Continuous operations for Web-based applications ■ Interface with ASPs and ISPs to provide recoveries

Business Relationship Management

This process aims to act as a liaison between IT operations and customers, providing the contact point for service-level administration, services marketing, customer satisfaction, and ongoing customer communications.

Automation	Stability
1 2 3 4 5 6 7 8 9 10 Manual Automatic	1 2 3 4 5 6 7 8 9 10 Dynamic Stable

Tasks	Skills
■ Interact with customers regarding questions/problems/requirements ■ Define tenets of service-level agreements ■ Translate business needs into IT support service fulfillment ■ Perform regular customer satisfaction reviews ■ Tie customer satisfaction to IT planning activities ■ Identify IT priorities based on customer feedback ■ Monitor results of help-desk support ■ Define processes and procedures for business relationship management	■ Strong communications skills ■ Ability to address both IT and business issues

Staffing	Automation Technology
❏ Business relationship manager ❏ Business/IT liaison ❏ Customer account representative	❏ Service level management/ reporting tools ❏ Customer satisfaction survey "application" ❏ Automated project/plan management tools

Best Practices	Metrics
❐ Identify primary point of contact for customers	❐ Customer satisfaction survey results
❐ Business relationship manager is clearly accountable for customer satisfaction	❐ Service-level attainment
	❐ Cost versus value comparisons for IT services
❐ Business relationship manager participates in IT/business planning processes	
❐ Process for improving customer service is iterative	
❐ Business relationship manager identifies new and improved services to customers	

Process Integration	Futures
■ No Items	■ Business relationship manager plays a leading role in IT project prioritization
	■ Business relationship manager oversees help-desk service and results
	■ Business relationship manager defines new customer-oriented metrics for measuring improvement

Capacity Planning

This process aims to predict future resource requirements and provide a capacity plan for all environments. This process involves gathering and analyzing forecast data from customers, trend analysis of historical data, and workload modeling to predict outcome of growth and upgrades.

Automation	Stability
1 2 3 4 5 6 7 **8** 9 10 Manual Automatic	1 2 **3** 4 5 6 7 8 9 10 Dynamic Stable

Tasks	Skills
■ Define processes for determining capacity requirements 1–2 years out	■ Understanding of key platform, operating-system, and subsystem components
■ Develop equipment plan and associated cost information	■ Understanding system measurement data
■ Recommend workload balancing options to avoid upgrades	■ Basic knowledge of statistical analysis
■ Identify individual components (such as memory and cache) to improve performance and thus eliminate/avoid upgrades	■ Understand performance characteristics for all resources
	■ Working knowledge of system/subsystem (such as I/O subsystems) tuning

Staffing	Automation Technology
❏ Capacity planner	❏ Capacity planning software (for example, BMC, IBM, Compuware, and others)
❏ Statistical analyst	❏ Statistical trend analysis
❏ Operations research analyst	❏ Simulation tools
	❏ Analytical modeling tools
	❏ Operating-system support utilities

Best Practices

❏ Common organization and management process for all capacity evaluations

❏ Occasional, temporary use of additional resources

❏ Proactive evaluation of all resources

❏ Ongoing tracking of actual versus planned usage by environment and by customer

❏ Tie-in to performance management processes

❏ Service-level attainment

❏ Bulk purchases (for example, on a quarterly basis) for cost-effectiveness

❏ Selective out-tasking of activities to third-party providers

❏ Use of simple business metrics where feasible

❏ Map of capacity requirements onto application infrastructure patterns

Metrics

❏ IT planned versus actual utilization

❏ Customer forecast versus actual

❏ Number and size of unplanned system acquisitions

Process Integration

■ Performance management

Futures

■ Capacity on demand

■ Cross-platform/domain modeling

■ Integration of service-level and performance processes

Change Management

This process aims to expedite change while minimizing business risk. It rationalizes changed impact, sets IT organizational change policies, and coordinates all changes to systems, networks, and applications.

Automation	Stability
1 2 **3** 4 5 6 7 8 9 10 Manual Automatic	1 **2** 3 4 5 6 7 8 9 10 Dynamic Stable

Tasks	Skills
■ Maintain ongoing process of accepting requests, analyzing them, submitting to management, and processing according to feedback ■ Develop integrated processes for all aspects of change management ■ Ensure that back-out provisions exist for all changes ■ Provide reasonable technical orientation to assess changes and back-outs	■ Strong process orientation/discipline ■ Detail oriented ■ Familiar with all major operational disciplines ■ Relationship/arbitration skills (people skills) ■ Familiarity with existing inventory and trouble ticketing systems

Staffing	Automation Technology
❐ Change specialist ❐ Change coordinator ❐ Impact assessment specialist ❐ Business/IT liaison	❐ Configuration management and infrastructure change/service request management tools ❐ Change management systems or add-ons such as Peregrine, HP, Tivoli, IBM ❐ Application change management (often focused more on configuration rather than change, such as CA-Endevor, ChangeMan, MicroFocus/InterSolv, Rational Atria, Continuus, and others) ❐ Vendor proprietary products, such as SAP CTS

Best Practices

- ❏ Building your own/internal application currently, but shifting to vendor tools
- ❏ Tends to break across software configuration management and infrastructure change/service request management tools
- ❏ Change management systems or add-ons, such as Peregrine, HP, Tivoli, IBM, and others
- ❏ Application change management (often focused more on configuration rather than change, such as CA Endevor, ChangeMan, MicroFocus/InterSolv, Rational Atria, Continuus, and others)
- ❏ Vendor proprietary, such as SAP CTS

Metrics

- ❏ Number of requests for change (RFCs)
- ❏ Proportion of RFCs rejected
- ❏ Gross numbers of changes and trends
- ❏ Percent of system outages with change as the root cause
- ❏ Percent of changes scheduled that are executed on time
- ❏ Percent of changes executed outside of normal change release schedule (that is, emergency changes)
- ❏ Number of changes backed out
- ❏ Number of support calls generated by executed changes
- ❏ Proportion of implemented changes that were unsuccessful

Process Integration

- ■ No Items

Futures

- ■ Development of quality-of-service metrics
- ■ Introduction of cost-recovery methodologies
- ■ New, more user-friendly technology

Configuration Management

Configuration management provides enterprise-wide, real-time component information (about hardware, software, networking, and other infrastructure) and incorporates new resources as required. In addition, it provides historical information.

Automation	Stability
1 2 3 4 5 6 7 8 9 10 Manual Automatic	1 2 3 4 5 6 7 8 9 10 Dynamic Stable
Tasks	**Skills**
■ Define configurations for all upgrade requests ■ Eliminate older technology when appropriate ■ Optimize access and connectivity for all configurations ■ Educate "customers" as to limitations of technology ■ Maximize flexibility and provide "growth room"	■ Knowledge of physical and architectural limitations for all devices ■ Knowledge of IT infrastructure ■ Understanding of automated configuration systems
Staffing	**Automation Technology**
❏ Configuration specialist ❏ Workload planning analyst ❏ Facilities planner	❏ Network configurations (such as CONTEL) ❏ System configurations (vendor-supplied)

Best Practices	Metrics
❐ New hardware configurations created automatically ❐ Integration of new technology and infrastructure specified automatically	❐ Cost/change ❐ Cost/inventory ❐ Group costs/configuration value

Process Integration	Futures
■ No Items	■ Configuration tools that include all enterprise devices within the same model ■ Built-in performance tolerances for specific configurations ■ Self-configuring automation based on technology parameters

Contract Management

Contract management handles contract design, negotiation, formalization, and inventory of contract terms and conditions to ensure that the company's needs are best served. It also requires work the development of strategies for asset acquisition and disposal.

Automation	Stability
1 2 3 4 5 6 7 8 9 10 Manual Automatic	1 2 3 4 5 6 7 8 9 10 Dynamic Stable

Tasks	Skills
■ Maintain all IT contracts ■ Evaluate terms and conditions to maximize corporate advantage ■ Develop and modify contracts for new/existing vendors ■ Provide regular status of contracts to IT management	■ Paralegal skills for contracts ■ Basic IT background in all major enterprise resources ■ Knowledge of lease and amortization processes ■ Ability to cull information from asset-tracking systems

Staffing	Automation Technology
❏ Contract specialist ❏ Financial analyst ❏ Administration specialist	❏ Asset-tracking systems ❏ Automatic contract storage, retrieval, and search engines

Best Practices	Metrics
❏ Automated systems that map contracts to IT components ❏ Aggressive contract negotiations a part of data center operations	❏ Cost/contract ❏ Group cost/number of contracts in place (and new)

Process Integration	Futures
■ No Items	■ Fully integrated, cross-platform systems for contracts that map to enterprise-wide asset tracking systems

Contractor Management

This process manages the activities and deliverables of all IT vendors as they relate to products and services. It is similar to the functions of a business relationship manager, but is directed toward vendors to the IT organization.

Automation	Stability
1 2 3 4 5 6 7 8 9 10 Manual Automatic	1 2 3 4 5 6 7 8 9 10 Dynamic Stable

Tasks	Skills
■ Coordinate activities with internal IT groups	■ Understanding of vendors and vendor deliverables
■ Define communications channels for each contractor	■ Ability to manage projects with minimal supervision
■ Define processes/procedures for contractor management	■ Ability to optimize added value from vendors/contractors
■ Eliminate unnecessary processes put in place by vendors	
■ Determine appropriate level of vendor involvement in IT projects	

Staffing	Automation Technology
❏ Vendor specialist	❏ Extensions to various asset-management tools
❏ Relationship managers	
❏ Project coordinator/manager	❏ Miscellaneous project-management tools
❏ Hardware/software specialist	
❏ Service delivery manager	❏ Excel spreadsheets

Best Practices	Metrics
❏ Use of a single approach and process for all vendors and contractors ❏ Use of work statements and other communication to define the role of contractors accurately	❏ Number of contracts/staff ❏ Number of projects/staff ❏ Project results (number of errors, delays)

Process Integration	Futures
■ No Items	■ Highly automated process for dealing with contractors (similar to internal management processes) ■ Defined processes for vendor interaction within IT ■ Establishment of vendor risk/reward for each major activity

Cost Recovery

This process provides a cost-accounting framework that maps the costs of components and other resources to drivers and customers.

Automation	Stability
1 **2** 3 4 5 6 7 8 9 10	1 2 3 4 5 6 **7** 8 9 10
Manual Automatic	Dynamic Stable

Tasks

- Develop cost centers and rates for 100% cost recovery
- Define processes/procedures for submitting forecasts
- Develop financial models to perform what-if rate scenarios
- Abide by generally accepted cost-accounting principles
- Utilize costing metrics

Skills

- Infrastructure knowledge
- Financial planning and cost management

Staffing

- ❏ Charge-back specialist
- ❏ Budget analyst
- ❏ Cost accounting specialist

Automation Technology

- ❏ Automated utilization collection systems (such as CA, Merrill Associates, Komand)
- ❏ Charge-back tools (such as Komand, CA, IBM)

Best Practices	Metrics

Best Practices

❐ Deployment of fully automated cost-recovery and rate-generation system

❐ Use of charge-back pricing methods with the following attributes:

❐ Understandable to users

❐ Predictable for planning purposes

❐ Related to value received

❐ Priced competitively with open market services

■ Use of one of the two models common today within user organizations:

    – Central pool allocated back to LOBs based upon revenue or employees

    – Usage-based pricing allocated directly to users/LOBs

Metrics

❐ Group cost/cost pools

❐ Degree of accuracy in actual recoveries

Process Integration

■ No Items

Futures

■ Automated cost-recovery modeling systems

■ Dynamically adjusting systems that factor in unplanned events to adjust recovery rates

Data Storage Management

This process aims to assure optimal use of storage resources and reduce long-term storage-unit cost by improving performance through policies for availability, location, and versioning; keeping enough (but not too much) storage available on the floor and providing backup/recovery operations for critical data; and by data-set placement and compaction.

Automation	Stability
1 2 3 4 5 6 7 **8** 9 10 Manual Automatic	1 2 3 4 5 6 7 **8** 9 10 Dynamic Stable

Tasks	Skills
■ Test/verify backup/restore versions ■ Maintain access and integrity of all corporate data on disk/DASD ■ Deploy compression/compaction utilities ■ Implement storage management automation tools ■ Assess appropriate level of RAID technology ■ Institute hierarchical storage management procedures ■ Evaluate storage performance trade-offs (disk placement, cache control)	■ Experience with storage area networking configuration and management ■ Knowledge of key vendors: EMC, Hitachi Data Systems, IBM

Staffing	Automation Technology
❑ Storage management specialist ❑ DASD specialist ❑ Backup/recovery specialist	❑ Storage area networks ❑ Storage systems ❑ Backup and recovery ❑ Storage management

Best Practices

- ❏ A validated tested backup/recovery system is in place
- ❏ A consolidated storage management architecture that is completely cross-platform
- ❏ Up-to-date backup and recovery plans for which all applications have been prioritized based on business-driven recovery requirements, including a list of what should be recovered and how long it should take
- ❏ Ongoing, regularly scheduled performance management/ optimization plan that includes determining which databases should be reorganized next, which volumes should be compressed/ compacted next, and figuring the maximum utilization that also minimizes the risk of application failures due to space allocation

Metrics

- ❏ Time to restore/recover/backup
- ■ Year-to-year improvements in:
  - – Utilization
  - – Cost/GB
  - – Staffing/unit capacity (staffing/ terabyte)
  - – Mean-time-between-failures: How many applications were affected how often, and for how long?

Process Integration

- ■ Tape management

Futures

- ■ Point-in-time replication deployed across enterprise to eliminate the need for batch and preventative maintenance windows
- ■ Storage technology improvements, including:
  - – Storage area networks
  - – Network attached storage
  - – Media commoditization lowering the price of storage devices
  - – Intelligent storage controllers and managers who understand characteristics of data and its usage, and automate decisions about where data is stored

Facilities Management

This process aims to keep the facilities that house and support IT operations running correctly. It seeks to eliminate single points of failure and to continuously maintain and upgrade the facilities to keep them at the level required by agreed-to levels of performance and availability.

Automation	Stability
1 2 **3** 4 5 6 7 8 9 10 Manual Automatic	1 2 3 4 5 6 7 8 **9** 10 Dynamic Stable

Tasks	Skills
■ Facilities evaluation ■ Network analysis ■ Space planning ■ Systems planning	■ Knowledge of architectural design ■ Engineering experience in specialties, including civil, communications, electrical, mechanical/HVAC, fire protection, security

Staffing	Automation Technology
❐ Facilities manager ❐ Space planner ❐ Site planner	❐ Configuration-modeling tools ❐ Homegrown

Best Practices	**Metrics**
❏ Use of third-party outsource providers	■ Year-to-year improvements in:
❏ Use of a single organization and a uniform process for enterprise-wide facilities management	– Staffing/major resource requests
	– Number of service / maintenance requests
❏ Methods for reducing single points of failure at the facilities level, e.g., redundant sources of electrical power, redundant connections for internetworking	– Time to service requests
	– Actual availability of facilities

Process Integration	**Futures**
■ No Items	■ Facilities technology improvements
	■ Higher availability (24×7×365)
	■ Increased redundancy of external utilities (e.g., power, communication
	■ Greater modularity and flexibility of base facility

Inventory Management

This process aims to provide detailed, accurate, real-time information listing the type, quantity, and location of all IT components.

Automation	Stability
1 2 3 **4** 5 6 7 8 9 10 Manual Automatic	1 2 **3** 4 5 6 7 8 9 10 Dynamic Stable

Tasks	Skills
■ Use automation (auto discovery) and manual procedures for maintaining full corporate IT inventory ■ Integrate inventory information with asset management, configuration management, and personnel management systems ■ Develop ways to identify inventory opportunities (such as unused items)	■ Basic understanding of corporate hardware/software ■ Ability to use automated inventory gathering and tracking tools ■ Use of both internal and external cost systems

Staffing	Automation Technology
❒ Inventory specialist ❒ Asset specialist ❒ Contract specialist ❒ Configuration specialist	❒ Tracking tools ❒ Auto-discovery tools such as SNMP

Best Practices	Metrics
❒ Use of real-time information systems for all IT inventories ❒ Use of automatic warnings regarding lease expirations and other life-cycle events	❒ Group costs/inventory costs ❒ Transaction/portfolio exchange costs ❒ Number of defects in configurations produced

Process Integration	Futures
■ No Items	■ More automation that includes portfolio analysis to evaluate whether it is feasible to swap out older resources for newer components with a lower cost and higher performance

Job Scheduling

This process aims to implement and maintain job schedules for all production and special production workloads. It includes interacting with customers to determine requirements, evaluating run-time requirements in relation to existing workloads, and ensuring timely completion—both in relation to the application itself and its neighbors in the execution queue.

Automation	Stability
1 2 3 4 5 6 7 **8** 9 10 Manual Automatic	1 2 3 **4** 5 6 7 8 9 10 Dynamic Stable

Tasks	Skills
■ Develop schedules for all corporate workloads ■ Perform "what-if" scheduling simulations as required ■ Evaluate and maximize workload balancing options ■ Define processes for changes and new submissions	■ Understanding of application system flow, including all aspects of input, output, and cross-application dependencies ■ Familiarity with the performance characteristics of all storage media (tape, disk, and so forth) and how they apply to processing of various workload types ■ Expertise in using various scheduling tools, including schedulers, simulation tools, and accounting systems for run-time analysis

Staffing	Automation Technology
❏ Scheduling coordinator ❏ Workload analyst	❏ Host-based schedulers ❏ Distributed schedulers ❏ Platform-specific schedulers

Best Practices

❐ Use of a single scheduling tool across the enterprise

❐ Use of a dynamically adjusting schedule based on self-analysis

❐ Integration of job scheduling with workload management and other policy-based management tools

❐ Periodic review of actual versus scheduled run-times

❐ Use of enhanced policy-based schedulers that enable customers (or application areas) to define parameters for scheduling

Metrics

❐ Percent of jobs meeting schedule

❐ Number of errors in defining schedule parameters

❐ Number of emergency scheduling needs/requests

❐ Average time to respond to new requests

❐ Staffing metrics

❐ Number of jobs/processes per analyst

Process Integration

■ Workload monitoring

Futures

■ Integration of service-level agreements and objectives with job schedulers

■ Policy-based scheduling systems for all IT resources

Negotiation Management

This process aims to negotiate the best terms with all vendors and to provide negotiation skills and a framework for ongoing interaction with IT suppliers.

Automation	Stability
1 2 3 4 5 6 7 8 9 10 Manual Automatic	1 2 3 4 5 6 7 8 9 10 Dynamic Stable
Tasks	**Skills**

■ Manage contract negotiations with hardware, software, and service providers
 	
 ■ Align service levels with business objectives
 	
 ■ Create favorable contractual terms for the IT organization
	■ Strong understanding of IT strategy and external IT market
	
	 ■ Understanding of industry best practices in negotiating:
	
	     – For each major vendor
	
	     – Corporate rules for each vendor
	
	 ■ Ability to integrate technological, financial, and legal information needed for successful negotiations

Staffing	**Automation Technology**
❑ Vendor manager ❑ Contract specialist ❑ Contract administrator	❑ Electronic access to legal, technological, supplier, and market information

Best Practices	Metrics
❒ Strong integration of negotiation management with the contract management process ❒ Ability to negotiate with vendors whose products are commodities (i.e., vary only in price, not functionality) and therefore whose margins are small	❒ Percent of discount versus industry average ❒ Scope of negotiation ❒ Number of enterprise-wide versus customer specific contracts ❒ Multi-year versus one-time iterations

Process Integration	Futures
■ Contract management	■ Improved, automated mapping of IT requirements to market and technology trends

Network Management

This process aims to provide reliable networking. It does this through continuous and consistent knowledge of network availability and health. It uses automated monitoring of all network resources, automated correlation of data, automatic notification of trouble, and rapid diagnosis and resolution of network availability problems.

Automation	Stability
1 2 **3** 4 5 6 7 8 9 10 Manual Automatic	1 2 3 **4** 5 6 7 8 9 10 Dynamic Stable

Tasks	Skills
■ Provide first-level network support using selected tool-sets	■ Familiarity with networking protocols and topology
■ Evaluate health of network and perform level one analysis	■ Understanding of SNA and IP network protocols
■ Define the processes and procedures for network monitoring	■ Knowledge of IP and SNMP
■ Enforce network usage standards—bandwidth requirements	■ Knowledge of network devices and relationships
■ Monitor OLTP and other transactional systems from a network view	

Staffing	Automation Technology
❒ Network control specialist	❒ Embedded instrumentation in network equipment (SNMP-based)
❒ Online systems specialist	
❒ Network support products (such as enterprise management tools)	❒ Network management platforms
	❒ OEM tool
	❒ Correlation tools
	❒ Configuration tools
	❒ Service-level management tools

Best Practices

- ❏ Highly automated network monitoring systems in place
- ❏ Integrated presentation of network status information to differing operational groups
- ❏ Use of monitoring to drive automation, notification, and problem management applications
- ❏ Ongoing documentation and evaluation of network topology, performance, standards, configuration, change control, faults, and accounting.

Metrics

- ❏ Ratio of personnel versus infrastructure elements (such as IP addresses)
- ❏ Percent of events processed automatically
- ❏ Network up-time (availability), component availability
- ❏ Network latency, data delivery rate, throughput
- ❏ Number of chronic problem groupings
- ❏ Mean time to isolate a link failure, repair it, and restore service

Process Integration

- ■ Configuration management
- ■ Problem management

Futures

- ■ Better assessment of business operational impact of network problems
- ■ Consolidation all resource-centric data (event, problem, asset, change)
- ■ Directory-enabled network management (for example, directories with policy content to drive quality of service tuning of network flows)
- ■ Better discovery technology for deriving device relationships

Output Management

This process aims at timely delivery of computer-generated output to appropriate distribution devices or users.

Automation	Stability
1 2 3 4 5 6 7 8 **9** 10 Manual Automatic	1 2 3 4 5 6 **7** 8 9 10 Dynamic Stable

Tasks	Skills
■ Operation of various output technologies ■ Output management software tools ■ Interface to mail room and interoffice delivery ■ Burst, sort, and de-leave operations ■ Restart/rerun of output as required ■ Use of print utilities to reproduce output as needed ■ Routing of output to various locations ■ Evaluate appropriateness of output medium ■ Identify ways to eliminate hardcopy print ■ Lower cost by using alternative media	■ Understanding of user needs ■ Understanding of system configuration

Staffing	Automation Technology
❒ Print operator ❒ Output manager	❒ Output management software ❒ Print protocols

Best Practices	Metrics
❐ Using a single output management process for the enterprise	❐ Cost/printed page normalized for media fluctuations
❐ Integration of print, output, and document management functions	❐ Percent of decrease in internal use hardcopy output
❐ Decentralized output processing to departments where possible	❐ Number of lost or missing outputs
❐ Benchmark annually to evaluate competitiveness of output operations with competitors, industry standards	❐ Number of reruns to reproduce lost/ damaged output
❐ Systematic reduction of hardcopy output	❐ Stratified cost structure for hard copy, electronic, departmentally printed, fiche, and optical output options

Process Integration	Futures
■ Integration of print, output, and document management	■ Integration of output with tape/ storage subsystems
	■ Customer-defined parameters for delivery, copies, frequency
	■ Common output management software for the enterprise
	■ Built-in archival based on business continuity/criticality
	■ Increased use of color technology

Performance Management

The aim of this process is to manage and maintain end-to-end performance for all workloads and environments.

Automation	Stability
1 2 3 4 5 6 **7** 8 9 10 Manual Automatic	1 2 3 4 5 6 7 **8** 9 10 Dynamic Stable

Tasks	Skills
■ Analyze performance of IT systems, storage, and networks ■ Define processes and procedures for performance management ■ Define thresholds and rules of thumb for optimal performance	■ Knowledge of all application processes and relationships ■ Ability to utilize performance tools ■ Understand performance of infrastructure components ■ Ability to adjust tuning parameters within each environment

Staffing	Automation Technology
❏ Performance analyst ❏ Systems tuning specialist ❏ Network optimization specialist	❏ Performance-monitoring tools ❏ Application-modeling tools ❏ Performance diagnostic tools ❏ All major operating systems, databases, transaction-processing subsystems, and hardware assist features (such as caching)

Best Practices

❐ Use of a common organization and performance-management process for all enterprise environments

❐ Development and maintenance of a mapping of business systems to performance patterns, using the following categories (patterns):

– Systems requiring sub-second transaction response time

– Collaborative systems

– Decision-support systems

– Systems supporting remote users

– Batch operations

❐ Integration of performance management with production acceptance process

❐ Use of policy-based objectives in the form of:

– Workload managers

– Service-level agreements

Metrics

❐ Consistent and repeatable:

– CPU service times

– Response times

– Batch turnaround

– Decision-support systems/ database applications response times

❐ Continuous improvement in achieving performance service levels

❐ Continuous improvement in performance processes

Process Integration

■ Capacity planning
■ Problem management

Futures

■ Dynamic (self-analyzing) tuning by application and cross-environments

■ Simulation/modeling of performance expectations for each of the seven patterns

■ Predictive performance problem identification

Problem Management

The aim of this process is to minimize the resolution time for problems by logging, tracking, and expediting problems as they occur, keeping stakeholders current as to resolution status, exploring all factors that can lower *mean time to resolution* (MTTR) and maintain a high level of overall customer satisfaction.

Automation	Stability
1 2 **3** 4 5 6 7 8 9 10 Manual Automatic	1 2 3 **4** 5 6 7 8 9 10 Dynamic Stable

Tasks	Skills
■ Escalate problems according to documented procedures	■ Detail-oriented with key relationship-management skills
■ Assess and resolve problems incurred among desktop, middle-tier, and mainframe systems (and associated networks)	■ Understand escalation and points of responsibility
■ Define processes and procedures for automated problem management	■ Expertise with the enterprise problem-management tools
■ Optimize problem-management techniques	
■ Ensure proper tracking and documentation for all problems	
■ Assure that help-desk policy is followed	

Staffing	Automation Technology
❐ Help-desk specialist ❐ Service manager	❐ None

Best Practices

❏ Provide problem management with a full-service help desk that has a single point of control in the enterprise. Move on from the legacy dispatch center and its associated problem desk. (For more information, consult the discussion of the customer advocacy COE.)

❏ Create and communicate a well-articulated vision and mission statement for the help desk

❏ Create a supported products list and communicate that list to clients

❏ Define points of escalation and delineate clear roles and responsibilities for next-level support groups

❏ Integrate the help desk into the IT value chain and promote proactivity. Act as the voice of the user in IT

❏ Maintain communication with all stakeholder groups: customers, IT managers, and help-desk employees

❏ Create an action plan

Metrics

❏ Customer satisfaction surveys

❏ Average help-desk queue time

❏ Average number call abandonment

❏ Average first-call resolution rates

❏ Mean time to resolution (MTTR)

❏ Mean time to response

❏ Support staff per 1000 supported users

Process Integration

■ No Items

Futures

■ Improved systems that are self-healing

■ Increased use of the Web to support user help

Production Acceptance

This process aims at defining and enforcing criteria for the release and migration of new and modified applications into the production environment. It works with the application developers to facilitate migration by ensuring that life-cycle milestones are achieved and by evaluating standards compliance in the applications.

Automation	Stability
1 2 3 **4** 5 6 7 8 9 10 Manual Automatic	1 **2** 3 4 5 6 7 8 9 10 Dynamic Stable

Tasks	Skills
■ Understand application development life cycle (ADLC) ■ Apply testing tools, such as simulation and modeling tools and load generation tools ■ Coordinate testing and upgrades between application areas and technical support/operations staff ■ Define requirements for successful completion ■ Develop documentation (with customers) to support operational requirements ■ Receive scheduling criteria for input to production schedules	■ Understanding must-have requirements—educating customers as to what is needed and why

Staffing	Automation Technology
❏ Production acceptance specialist ❏ Application liaison ❏ Life-cycle specialist	❏ Testing tools ❏ Life-cycle software ❏ Documentation tools for application processing

Best Practices	Metrics
❐ Use a common acceptance procedure across the enterprise	❐ Average time to production acceptance (by complexity)
❐ Use a production acceptance "lab" mirroring infrastructure	❐ Number of unsuccessful/partially failed applications implemented
❐ Define must-have requirements for any application that will be turned over to operations	❐ Number of reverted deployments
	❐ Number of errors in scheduling new applications
❐ Halt deliverables unless all requirements are met	❐ Time to estimate infrastructure cost of new applications (PCM model)
❐ Automate sign-off processes throughout the application development life cycle (ADLC)	❐ Average time to respond to new requests
	❐ Staffing metrics
❐ Modify the ADLC to handle shorter development cycles enabled by packaged software solutions	❐ Number of applications accepted/ analyst

Process Integration	Futures
■ No Items	■ New production acceptance methods, as follows:
	– Integrated, enterprise-wide software configuration management
	– User interfaces for application developers that require conformance to ADLC checkpoints
	■ Increased use of third-party service providers in the production assurance process

Production Control

This process aims at assuring production integrity (often via audits) of the production-acceptance process and job-scheduling functions.

Automation	Stability
1 2 **3** 4 5 6 7 8 9 10 Manual Automatic	1 2 **3** 4 5 6 7 8 9 10 Dynamic Stable

Tasks	Skills
■ Notify programmers of problems with jobs/transactions ■ Define processes supporting production-acceptance process	■ Familiarity with restart/recovery procedures for production workloads ■ Attention to detail ■ Understanding of production-environment sequences and mapping to business cycles ■ Understand business checks, balances, and data tolerances

Staffing	Automation Technology
❐ Production coordinator ❐ CL/script specialist ❐ IOB liaison	❐ Production control software ❐ Report-balancing software

Best Practices

❏ A uniform method for handling production control across the enterprise

❏ A focus on workflow processes to ensure comprehensive management without encumbering clients

❏ Systems that integrate scheduling tools and performance-management (policy-based) software

❏ A focus on minimizing defects based on continuous improvement of testing and life-cycle processes

❏ Development of an ongoing schedule of application optimization

❏ A production control method that addresses electronic commerce, ERP, CRM, and other production processes

❏ A production method that integrates software configuration management processes to data center change processes

Metrics

❏ Number of failed applications/month

❏ Mean time to resolution

❏ Number of scheduling errors and invalid run-time projections

❏ Number of applications accepted without proper documentation/testing, and so forth

❏ Average time for handling application change requests, by request type

Process Integration

■ Production acceptance

Futures

■ New application-management technologies

■ Integrated, enterprise-wide software configuration management

■ Intelligent scheduling tools

■ Self-healing applications and databases (automated tuning)

■ Use of third-party service providers for production control

Physical Database Management

This process aims to manage the physical design, integrity, performance, and access to corporate database systems. It assists customers with implementation of database redesign, optimization, and recovery activities.

Automation	Stability
1 2 3 4 5 6 7 8 9 10 Manual Automatic	1 2 3 4 5 6 7 8 9 10 Dynamic Stable

Tasks	Skills
■ Utilize database management software tools ■ Utilities to extract, duplicate, and back up databases ■ Define and enforce standards around database design/usage ■ Support ad hoc requests for temporary databases	■ Understand physical characteristics of the major database vendors ■ Knowledgeable about the redesign, optimization, and recovery of database elements

Staffing	Automation Technology
❐ Storage administrators ❐ Storage management specialists ❐ Database specialist	❐ Database management software ❐ Support utilities for reorganization, data-set extraction, backup, and so forth

Best Practices	Metrics
❏ Use of a common organization and management process for all enterprise databases ❏ Proactive monitoring of databases for optimization ❏ Interface with Disk Storage Management process to ensure appropriate media selection and caching approach ❏ Achieving appropriate availability for production databases	❏ Cost/MB of database data ❏ Database availability ❏ Response time ❏ Mean time to recovery

Process Integration	Futures
■ Disk management	■ Self-analyzing database design software ■ Tighter integration of databases and storage subsystems ■ Policy-based management software ■ Mirroring/vaulting technologies for continuous operations ■ Better understanding of responsibilities for shared data among businesses

Quality Assurance

This process aims to establish, support, and enforce corporate quality standards associated with every process in the company. It is deeply involved with acceptance testing, and it performs audits of applications, infrastructure, and life-cycle procedures. It also tracks trending of tolerance levels for operations.

Automation	Stability
1 2 **3** 4 5 6 7 8 9 10 Manual　　　　　　Automatic	1 2 3 4 5 6 **7** 8 9 10 Dynamic　　　　　　Stable

Tasks	Skills

■ Evaluate company processes for efficiency, practicability, and so on
■ Improve IT processes
■ Support IT people in each process
■ Evaluate workloads for production readiness
■ Ensure appropriate testing/ documentation prior to production release
■ Define quality-assurance processes for testing
■ Assess completeness of testing (both logic testing and the appropriateness of the test bed)
	■ Expertise in using:
	
	  – Simulation tools
	
	  – Quality-assurance tools
	
	  – Life-cycle tools and processes
	
	  – Trending tools
	
	■ Understanding of application system flow, including all aspects of input, output, and cross-application dependencies
	■ Familiarity with all corporate standards for quality assurance
	■ Development of new quality assurance standards for "new age" workloads

Staffing	Automation Technology
❐ Controller ❐ QA specialist ❐ Production coordinator ❐ LOB liaison	❐ QA tools

Best Practices

❐ Use of interactive tools that enable customers to participate directly in quality-assurance efforts

❐ Periodic reporting and enforcement of level of compliance

❐ Use of quality-assessment information to improve performance of application and infrastructure teams

Metrics

❐ Cost of quality (and non-quality)

❐ Customer satisfaction

❐ Number of failed processes

❐ Percent of jobs adhering to quality-assurance policies/standards

❐ Number of defects in applications that were compliant with quality-assurance principles

❐ Number of emergency quality-assurance review processes

❐ Average time to respond to new requests

❐ Number of jobs and processes per analyst

Process Integration

■ All processes

Futures

■ QA integrated across all centers of excellence

■ Automated tools for risk/complexity analysis

■ Defect discovery

Security Management

This process aims to assure IT security by granting and enforcing the appropriate level of access to applications and data to internal and external personnel through the use of day-to-day administration of security policies and the use of a consistent security policy across all enterprise resources.

Automation	Stability
1 2 **3** 4 5 6 7 8 9 10 Manual Automatic	1 2 3 4 5 6 **7** 8 9 10 Dynamic Stable

Tasks	Skills
■ Provide new user-ID password for customers ■ Reset passwords as required ■ Use automation to perform monitoring/administration tasks ■ Develop processes to improve security management processes	■ Understanding of all operational processes that deliver services and process interaction points ■ Expertise in service-level reporting tools ■ Knowledge of customer applications/systems ■ Understanding of cost/performance trade-offs ■ Ability to communicate well ■ Knowledge of security technologies and products

Staffing	Automation Technology
❒ Security administrator ❒ Security policy manager	❒ General network and systems management (NSM) tools for monitoring (that is, availability management) ❒ Reporting add-ons to general NSM tools ❒ Firewall and virtual private network products for perimeter defense; intrusion detection products for defense within perimeter ❒ Single sign-on and Kerberos products for efficient and secure use of password authentication

Best Practices	Metrics
❐ Use of single sign-on technologies to streamline user access while maintaining security	❐ Number of security breaches/time
	❐ Cost of security breaches/time
❐ Use of Kerberos-style tokens to avoid transmitting passwords over insecure networks	❐ Level of customer satisfaction (survey feedback)
	❐ Cost of administering/number of service-level agreements (and customers)
❐ Use of intrusion detection technologies within the boundaries of the enterprise	❐ Service availability
	❐ Service performance
❐ Service levels coupled to externalized metrics	❐ Service quality (QOS)
❐ End-to-end objectives reflecting business perception	

Process Integration	Futures
■ Most processes	■ End-to-end perspective
	■ End-user perspective
	■ Consolidated reporting
	■ Feedback of service metrics to control management policy
	■ "What if" analysis of suggested service-level agreements in relation to cost
	■ Stronger tie-in of cost/service trade-offs

Service-Level Management

This process aims to ensure consistent delivery of services and accurate reporting of agreed-to service levels. This process implies management to an optimized level of availability, performance, and quality.

Automation	Stability
1 **2** 3 4 5 6 7 8 9 10 Manual Automatic	1 2 3 4 5 6 **7** 8 9 10 Dynamic Stable

Tasks	Skills
■ Document, monitor and perform corrective action to manage service-level agreements ■ Define processes/procedures for management of service-level agreements	■ Understanding of all operational processes that deliver services and process interaction points ■ Expertise in service-level reporting tools ■ Knowledge of customer applications/systems ■ Understanding of cost/performance trade-offs ■ Ability to communicate well

Staffing	Automation Technology
❒ Business relationship manager ❒ Reporting specialist for service-level agreements ❒ Service-level manager	❒ General network and systems-management (NSM) tools for monitoring (for example, of availability management) ❒ Reporting add-ons to general NSM tools ❒ Data consolidation and reporting tools ❒ End-user perspective tools ❒ Problem management (help desk) reporting tools

Best Practices	Metrics
❒ Escalation process for negative feedback	❒ Parallel individual feedback loop (individual feedback form)
❒ Service levels coupled to externalized metrics	❒ Actual versus target service levels
❒ End-to-end objectives reflecting business focus	❒ Level of customer satisfaction (survey feedback)
❒ Use of automated service-level agreement reporting tools	❒ Cost of administering/number of service-level agreements (or customers)
❒ High level of automation of reporting	❒ Service availability
❒ Web-based customized service-level reporting	❒ Service performance
	❒ Service quality (QOS)

Process Integration	Futures
■ No items	■ End-to-end perspective
	■ End-user perspective
	■ Consolidated reporting
	■ Streamlined feedback of service metrics to control management policy
	■ What-if analysis of suggested service-level agreements in relation to cost
	■ Stronger tie-in of cost/service trade-offs

Service Request Management

This process aims to ensure the timely acceptance, documentation, handling, and close-out of service requests.

Automation	Stability
1 2 3 4 **5** 6 7 8 9 10 Manual Automatic	1 2 3 4 5 6 7 **8** 9 10 Dynamic Stable

Tasks	Skills
■ Accept service requests and document accordingly ■ Provide response according to pre-defined service-level requests ■ Evaluate scope of request and define work effort to user ■ Determine ways to better address core requirement because customers do not always know what they need ■ Define processes/procedures to improve request process	■ Attention to details ■ Knowledge of service-level agreement approach to IT management

Staffing	Automation Technology
❏ Help-desk specialist ❏ Line of business liaison ❏ Customer service representative	❏ Various point products to manage service requests ❏ Help-desk tools

Best Practices	Metrics
❐ Management with clearly defined categories for service-level requests ❐ Strictly defined service-level agreements for each category ❐ Automated process enabling customers to enter service requests ❐ Automated escalation of overdue requests	❐ Number of requests/month ❐ Number of requests/staff ❐ MTTR for each request (by type) ❐ Number of late service events/ number of requests

Process Integration	Futures
■ Job scheduling	■ Increased automation to enable quicker and cheaper management of servicing requests ■ Fully automated SR process ■ Ongoing improvement in the descriptions of service by type and escalation procedures

Software Distribution

This process aims at preparing, scheduling, and executing the distribution of software throughout the enterprise in a secure and expeditious manner. It works closely with the change and service request management capabilities in the IT organization.

Automation	Stability
1 2 3 4 **5** 6 7 8 9 10 Manual Automatic	1 2 3 4 5 6 **7** 8 9 10 Dynamic Stable

Tasks	Skills
■ Define deployment endpoints and software stack for software distribution with automation tools ■ Evaluate success of distributions ■ Execute fallback procedures if necessary ■ Define processes and procedures for optimizing enterprise software distribution process	■ Familiarity with configuration of target environments (such as registry, desktop structure, etc.) ■ Understanding of change management and inventory management processes ■ Expertise in chosen automation technology and products

Staffing	Automation Technology
❐ Production coordinator ❐ Software distribution specialist	❐ Microsoft Systems Management Server ❐ Novadigm EDM ❐ Tivoli Software Distribution ❐ CA Unicenter TNG Software Distribution/ShipIT ❐ IBM LCCM ❐ Novell ZENWorks ❐ Intel LANDesk ❐ Mobile user support: Callisto, Marimba, Mobile Automation, Sterling Software (Xcellnet)

Best Practices	Metrics
❏ Automated distribution of all major enterprise applications	❏ Number of discrete distributions performed weekly/monthly
❏ Minimal custom scripting of software distribution solutions	❏ MB/GB transferred per week/month
❏ Use of distribution tools that deliver to multi-tiered, multi-platform architectures	❏ Staff-per-target-resources ratio ❏ Staff-per-distributions ratio
❏ Tight integration between software distribution techniques and: – Change management – Configuration management – Inventory/asset management (distributions drive updates) – Problem management	

Process Integration	Futures
■ Change management ■ Configuration management ■ Inventory/asset management (distributions drive updates) ■ Problem management	■ Automated mirroring and end-user document version control (such as Microsoft Active Directory, Intellimirror) ■ Complexity stratification (browser-based, e-mail based, multi-tiered operating systems) ■ Increased support of mobile computing devices and technologies

System Monitoring

This process aims to provide continuous knowledge of systems availability, health, and status. It does so by monitoring all server, database, and application resources; responding to system and application-generated requests and events; automating monitored events; and rapidly diagnosing and resolving availability problems.

Automation	Stability
1 2 3 4 5 6 7 8 **9** 10 Manual Automatic	1 2 3 4 5 6 7 8 **9** 10 Dynamic Stable

Tasks	Skills
■ Monitor health of enterprise systems ■ Determine when problems exist and escalate as required ■ Ensure optimal availability, using predefined procedures to recover systems when problems occur ■ Define processes/procedures to optimize system monitoring process	■ Expertise with selected monitoring tools ■ Ability to determine Basic Level 1 problems ■ Knowledge of management protocols (such as SNMP) ■ Knowledge of component (operating system, databases, middleware, and so on) behavior

Staffing	Automation Technology
❏ Console specialist ❏ Systems operations specialist ❏ Availability specialist	❏ OEM-supplied tools ❏ Instrumentation ❏ Suites

Best Practices

- ❏ Extremely high level of automated monitoring
- ❏ Use of standard instrumentation provided by system suppliers
- ❏ Ability to integrate event data across processes
- ❏ Ability to integrate and present system information to differing operational groups
- ❏ Integration of system monitoring with automation, notification, and problem management systems
- ❏ Integration of event data with service-level agreement reporting
- ❏ Use of Web-based user access to system management data

Metrics

- ❏ Class and aggregate resource availability
- ❏ Number of elements monitored per employee
- ❏ Employees per 10,000 events
- ❏ Unit cost of monitoring per 10,000 events
- ❏ Percentage of events handled manually

Process Integration

- ■ Performance management
- ■ Problem management

Futures

- ■ Further consolidation of resource-centric data related to monitoring (event, problem, asset, change)
- ■ Additional cross-platform integration (and with console automation) into business process and application views
- ■ Derivative capabilities of business impact based on outages

Tape Management

This process manages and optimizes methods to allocate, store, administer, and optimize tape usage. It seeks to make sure that enough (but not too much) operational tape is available; that various tape media, including virtual tape, are used as effectively as possible; and that manual tape mounts are kept to a minimum.

Automation	Stability
1 2 3 4 **5** 6 7 8 9 10 Manual Automatic	1 2 3 4 5 6 7 8 **9** 10 Dynamic Stable

Tasks	Skills
■ Retrieve, mount, and replace tapes in tape library ■ Manage automated tape loaders, virtual tape, silos, and all major vendor technologies in the tape family ■ Manage tape systems with automation tools ■ Improve performance by tuning tape parameters, including block size, compression, and caching	■ Knowledge of utilities associated with copy, repair, and various production support processes ■ Basic understanding of tape library functions (retention, inventory, and so forth) ■ Understanding of storage performance trade-offs (disk versus tape, near-line versus offline) ■ Experience with storage area networking management

Staffing	Automation Technology
❏ None	❏ Tape transport subsystems ❏ Silos and virtual tape servers ❏ Tape-management software

Best Practices

❑ Use of a common organization and management process for tape storage systems across all platforms

❑ Maintenance of a detailed inventory and catalog mechanism for all tape files

❑ Use of automated software to manage business continuity tapes

❑ Use of automatic placement of data to manage performance based on data criticality, access frequency, and so forth

❑ Ongoing performance management/optimization process that monitors tapes coming up for expiration, length of service for each tape, and optimal file placement on tapes

❑ Ongoing investigation of how costs can be reduced both internally and externally

Metrics

❑ Utilization per cartridge

❑ Number of (manual) mounts

❑ Cost/GB (or cartridge)

❑ Staffing per unit capacity (staffing/n-tapes/mounts/etc.)

❑ Mean-time-between-failures (MTBF): How many applications were affected, and for how long, due to tape-related issues?

Process Integration

■ Disk storage management

Futures

■ Tape to become an element of a Storage Area Network

■ Virtual tape (data set indexing)

■ Transport independence

■ Inter-platform use of automated tape

■ Media commoditization

■ Intelligent storage controllers

■ Higher integration of tape and disk subsystems

■ Dynamic (and intelligent) data placement independent of media

Workload Monitoring

This process ensures consistent, stable, and predictable workflow cycles by monitoring all job streams for completion (and following up on job exceptions). It works with the Production Control process to optimize workflow and to facilitate the handling of ad hoc and emergency requests without disruption.

Automation	Stability
1 2 3 4 5 6 7 **8** 9 10 Manual　　　　　　Automatic	1 2 3 4 5 6 **7** 8 9 10 Dynamic　　　　　　Stable

Tasks	Skills
◼ Evaluate the health of specific jobs/workloads as assigned ◼ Expedite workload processing to ensure service-level agreement compliance ◼ Define ways to better improve monitoring processes/automation	◼ Attention to detail ◼ Ability to follow a methodology consistently ◼ Understanding of major, critical job streams and business functions that they support ◼ Expertise in operating environments and chosen automation tool(s)

Staffing	Automation Technology
❑ Console operator ❑ Systems operations specialist ❑ Production coordinator	❑ BMC Control-M/Enterprise Console System (ECS) ❑ CA-Unicenter TNG Workload Management, (PLAT) AutoSys, CA-Jobtrac, CA-Scheduler, CA-7, CA-Jobwatch, FAQS/PCS ❑ Cybermation ESP Workload Manager ❑ ISA AppWorx ❑ SEA CSAR ❑ SMA The Scheduler, OpCon/XPS ❑ Tivoli Workload Manager (Maestro), (IBM) OPC/ESA

Best Practices	**Metrics**
❐ High degree of workload monitoring automation	❐ Number of operators per 10,000 jobs
❐ Eventual elimination of all manual job "set-ups"	❐ Percent of jobs run on time
❐ Ability to monitor jobs scheduled on different operating platforms	❐ Number of ad hoc requests handled
❐ Integration of workload monitoring with event management	❐ Number of exceptions per 10,000 jobs

Process Integration	**Futures**
■ Production control	■ Additional automation
	■ Better cross-platform integration

Chapter 8

Center of Excellence Catalog

This catalog lists the COEs typically found at the most advanced IT organizations in large firms. The entries for each COE map to similar information provided for each process in the Process Catalog in Chapter 7.

Where product or company names appear, these entries do not represent endorsements, nor does the absence of a product or company imply that it is not recommended or useful. These mentions serve only to list some representative products.

As in Chapter 7, open bullets (❑) indicate items that you should compare with current processes at your site and mark those you have implemented.

Application Center

This COE aims to provide a stable and repeatable production environment, coupled with emergency acceptance procedures that comply with established information systems policies, quality assurance standards, procedures, and management practices.

Attributes	Processes
■ Area of expertise—Communicating application standards and policies through effective management of same on a day-to-day basis ■ Binding theme—Managing enterprise production workloads ■ Value proposition—Timely and quality output with minimal defects	❏ Quality assurance ❏ Production control/acceptance ❏ Job scheduling ❏ Application optimization ❏ Software distribution

Skills	Automation
❏ Have a broad understanding of the enterprise application infrastructure, with a detailed knowledge of tools necessary to diagnose and fix problems ❏ Knowledge of scheduling, job setup, data control, workflow changes, and postprocessing functions required by all systems to expedite the production cycles ❏ Ability to move modules/ executables from test to production libraries ❏ Ability to perform troubleshooting for failed jobs/processes ❏ Understanding of requirements and process for run-time setup, run documentation, and data files	❏ Scheduling systems (CA-7, CA-UNICENTER/TNG, OPC/ESA, etc.) ❏ Software change management (CA-Endevor, ChangeMan, LCM) ❏ Operations documentation ❏ Application optimization (Strobe, PPE)

Best Practices

- Rendering production handling common across the enterprise
- Adapting workflow processes to ensure comprehensive management without encumbering clients
- Having an effective emergency production acceptance process
- Developing "hooks" between scheduling tools and performance management (policy-based) software
- Minimizing defects based on continuous improvement of testing and life-cycle processes
- Developing an ongoing schedule of application optimization:
  - Which applications/when
  - Focus areas (DB, locality of reference)
  - Target metrics for improvement
- Addressing "new age" production processes such as EC, ERP, CRM
- Tying software-configuration management processes to data-center change processes

Metrics

- Percentage of jobs/processes meeting schedule
- Ratio of changes/availability
- Number of failed applications/month
- Mean time to resolution
- Number (or percentage) of people per change
- Unit cost per change
- Number of scheduling errors/invalid run-time projections
- Number of applications accepted without proper documentation and testing
- Average time for handling application change requests by request type
- Analysts/application
- Supervisors/analyst
- Schedulers/number of servers

Futures

- New application management technologies
  - Integrated, enterprisewide software-configuration management
  - Intelligent scheduling tools (load balancing)
  - Self-healing applications/databases (automated tuning)

- Automated quality control
- Automated performance and capacity analysis

Asset Center

This COE aims to provide optimization for all IT resources.

Attributes	Processes
■ Area of expertise—Procurement and financial management ■ Binding theme—IT asset portfolio ■ Value proposition—Asset utilization and unit-cost reduction	❑ Asset management ❑ Inventory management ❑ Contract management ❑ Contractor management ❑ Negotiations/portfolio management ❑ Cost-recovery management ❑ Budget management

Skills	Automation
❑ In-depth knowledge of IT asset characteristics, including associated technology metrics ❑ Knowledge in the areas of cost accounting, procurement, asset tracking/inventory tools/techniques ❑ Able to negotiate agreements ❑ Understanding of licensing and warranty terms and conditions	❑ Inventory collection/tracking ❑ Asset management tools ❑ Fixed-asset packages ❑ Budgeting and financial modeling tools ❑ Enterprise information systems/decision-support tools

Best Practices

❒ Full automation for each major process, with linkage between processes

❒ Common IT asset management across the enterprise

❒ Consolidated asset portfolio:

  – How many

  – Where everything is

  – Its current value

❒ Simple models for cost accounting that provide incentives for proper behavior

❒ Executing on clearly defined cost-reduction goals (year after year)

Metrics

❒ IT cost as percentage of corporate revenue/earnings

❒ Asset utilization by major resource category

❒ Appropriation and procurement processing performance

❒ Total cost per asset resource tracked

❒ Employees per 1,000 asset elements

❒ Long-term unit costs

Futures

■ CFO for IT

■ Real-time asset management

■ Automated financial accountability for assets, projects, and ongoing operations

■ Integration with capacity planning process

■ Factoring utilization of assets into procurements

■ Automated technology refresh

■ Integration with corporate fixed-asset tracking

Command Center

This COE aims to provide effective end-to-end, application-focused monitoring of the enterprise computing resources.

Attributes	Processes
■ Area of expertise—Application and infrastructure health ■ Binding theme—Real-time monitoring ■ Value proposition—Ensuring end-to-end availability and throughput	❐ Change management ❐ Performance management ❐ Configuration management ❐ Asset management ❐ Problem management

Skills	Automation

❐ Basic knowledge of things being monitored
  – Topology and how applications fit
  – Nature/severity of events relevant to what is being managed
❐ Familiar with workload management technology
❐ Understanding of server—SNMP or proprietary event mechanism
❐ Network—SNMP, RMON, RMON2
❐ Experience with automation tools: Languages, rules, filters, and so forth
	❐ SNMP Platforms—HP, IBM, Sun, Cabletron
	❐ Agentry
	  – Server-centric—BMC Patrol, CA/Platinum, Compuware
	  – Desktop-centric
	  – Network probes
	❐ Console consolidation and automation tools—CA-OPS/MVS, Candle AF-Operator, IBM NetView

Best Practices	Metrics

Best Practices

❐ Deliver true end-to-end availability and performance monitoring by application by user

❐ Extremely high degrees of automation indicated by:

   – Few staff members manually watching anything anymore

   – Most effort is focused on further automation so that even less watching need occur

   – New workloads (or changes in workloads) can rapidly be mapped into automated processes

❐ Use of outsourcers

Metrics

❐ Percentage system availability
❐ Performance (response time)
❐ Total number of jobs completed
❐ Percentage of jobs completed on schedule
❐ Staff/10,000 production jobs
❐ Staff/IP address
❐ Staff/used MIPS
❐ Cost/managed IP address
❐ Cost/10,000 jobs

Futures

■ Monitoring the end-user experience

■ Achieving end-to-end service-level views

■ Infrastructure commoditization— monitoring capability increasingly will be built into infrastructure (such as XML)

■ New applications that need to be monitored, such as electronic commerce

■ New technologies to monitor Web servers, middleware, storage-area networks

■ Outsourcing and out-tasking

Customer Advocacy Center

This COE aims to serve as the voice of customers to IT, and the voice of IT to customers.

Attributes	Processes
■ Area of expertise—Effective, full-range customer support	❏ Problem management
■ Binding theme—Customer satisfaction	❏ Business relationship management
	❏ Service-level management
■ Value proposition—Ensure that customer needs are met	❏ Service request management
	❏ Product/services marketing
	❏ Change management
	❏ Configuration management
	❏ Asset management

Skills	Automation
❏ Strong communication and interpersonal skills	❏ Problem management tools
	❏ Customer satisfaction surveys
❏ Strong business application knowledge	❏ Service-level reporting/management tools
❏ Ability to facilitate and prioritize	
❏ Base knowledge of all IT processes and infrastructure	
❏ Ability to focus on resolution	

Best Practices

❑ Consolidated single point of contact for all customer needs and problems

❑ Included in the customer's business planning process

❑ High degree of credibility in being the customer's advisor

❑ Compensation based on customer satisfaction throughout IT

Metrics

❑ Customer satisfaction by surveys

❑ Help-desk metrics (quality of service)

❑ Staff per 1,000 end users supported

Futures

■ Increasing percentage of compensation tied to business/ satisfaction metrics

■ Capabilities of measuring service impacts

■ Linking of customer satisfaction results to IT planning

Data and Media Center

This COE aims to cost-effectively ensure the integrity, availability, and security of enterprise data.

Attributes	Processes
■ Area of expertise—All forms of data and media management ■ Binding theme—Enterprise storage architecture ■ Value proposition—Providing common storage services across all platforms	❒ Disk storage management ❒ Tape storage management ❒ Output management (including fiche) ❒ Business continuity ❒ Physical database management

Skills	Automation
❒ Familiarity with all storage technologies (capabilities, limitations, performance characteristics), including utilities to perform reorganizations of data, backups, recoveries, extracts, and archive for disaster recovery ❒ Expertise in common storage-management tools ❒ Capability to perform basic tuning, placement, access (sharing)	❒ Policy-based storage management (SAMS: Vantage, SpaceView) ❒ Tape management (TLMS, CA-1, RMM) ❒ Database management (various DB2, Oracle, Sybase tools) ❒ Disaster-recovery management (Sunrise, Arise II)

Best Practices

❐ Shared technology access across platforms

❐ Enterprise management tools with a common interface

❐ Defined pattern-focused model for data placement that addresses availability, business continuity, performance, and capacity

❐ Automated, enterprise-wide hierarchical storage management

❐ Integration with production acceptance processes

❐ Specific requirements definition for disaster recovery across all critical systems

❐ DB management practices that ensure ongoing, proactive optimization

Metrics

❐ Cost/GB

❐ Cost/tape

❐ Cost/output unit (view/page)

❐ Staff/GB

❐ Staff/tape

❐ Staff/output unit

Futures

■ Storage-area networks (enterprise storage)

■ Integrated tape, disk, DASD, output management tools/processes

■ Selective out-tasking of commodity management roles

■ Adaptations to link external business partners/disaster-recovery sites

■ "New age" storage-management tools

■ Dynamic caching candidate identification/implementation

■ Self-healing I/O subsystems built into storage technologies

■ Introduction of the heterogeneous storage server

■ Integration of storage-management "intelligence" within DASD/tape controllers and heterogeneous servers

■ Common management of networked and legacy storage subsystems

Engineering Support Center

This COE aims to plan, implement, and support enterprise-wide infrastructure components in accordance with the enterprise-wide technical architecture. It focuses primarily on hardware (desktops/laptops, servers, and peripherals), networks (data and voice), software, middleware, and availability.

Attributes	Processes
■ Area of expertise—Technical expertise associated with each technology, its relationship to business applications, and the integration of infrastructure and business systems as needed	❑ Capacity management ❑ Database administration (physical) ❑ Middleware management ❑ Infrastructure planning ❑ Hardware support ❑ Software management (including network software) ❑ Test lab management
■ Binding theme—Establish and maintain infrastructure resources in the context of the enterprise-wide technical architecture	
■ Value proposition—Timely, leverageable, and quality technologies to meet business requirements	

Skills	Automation
❑ Knowledge of operating system, middleware, and subsystem components	❑ System tools ❑ Database management tools ❑ Various performance management/capacity planning tools ❑ Testing tools
❑ Ability to utilize tools for capacity planning	
❑ Current (general) knowledge of the enterprise-wide technical architecture and its components	
❑ Ability to implement/support security technologies	
❑ Understanding of life-cycle process and ability to support technical roles (such as testing, QA)	
❑ Technical understanding of popular database technologies	

Best Practices

- ❏ Standard software configuration for all similar platforms
- ❏ Cyclic approach to applying software maintenance
- ❏ Periodic review of actual versus capacity plan
- ❏ Established relationship between capacity and service-level attainment
- ❏ Interface to each nontechnical COE (with SLAs in place)
- ❏ Unified approach to addressing network (data/telecom) and server (system) support and maintenance
- ❏ Education to customers as to rules of engagement related to infrastructure implementation/ usage
- ❏ Clearly defined run documentation for operations groups
- ❏ Assistance in developing operational management policies

Metrics

- ❏ Percentage of successful implementations/upgrades
- ❏ Ratio of changes/availability
- ❏ Number of failed applications/ month
- ❏ Mean time to resolution for technical problems
- ❏ Number (or percentage) of people per operating system, image, networked user
- ❏ Unit cost per software change
- ❏ Database administrators per database/database technology
- ❏ Supervisors/systems programmer

Futures

- ■ Develop and maintain a map of both infrastructure and business software/technologies
- ■ Explicit career opportunities between technical support and operations

- ■ Provide full, enterprise-wide integration and reuse of all software, database, and other data for internal and external consumption

Outsourcing Center

This COE aims to reconcile business needs and vendor delivery. It coordinates company functions (such as procurement, business liaison, legal, financial) to specify, negotiate, and deliver company requirements.

Attributes	Processes
■ Area of expertise—Coordinating cross functional expertise toward central objective and results ■ Binding theme—Managing external vendors and integrating them to internal culture ■ Value proposition—Increased business value (cost reduction, time to market, or quality) from sourcing	❑ Procurement ❑ Contract management ❑ SLA measurement/management ❑ Governance/change management ❑ Asset management ❑ Legal administration ❑ Processes around activities outsourced

Skills	Automation
❑ Ability to liaise with business personnel to ensure coordination of services with business requirements ❑ Ability to act as ombudsman for vendor and manage vendor for corporation	❑ No direct automation tools; only indirect financial system and service-level agreement reporting to support personnel

Best Practices

❏ Use of service-level agreements and value scorecard for contribution of the group

❏ Sponsorship of process-improvement initiatives

❏ Regular focus on coordination among lines of business, customer satisfaction surveys, forecasts of requirements and new initiatives

Metrics

❏ Percentage of service-level agreement requirements met

❏ Customer satisfaction by survey

Futures

■ Increased alignment with business objectives as IT organizations improve ability to understand and align IT strategies

■ Formal organization within IT that tracks both internal service-level agreements and external performance to improve reconciliation of services

■ Increasing awareness by non-IT organizations that sourcing impacts business results and is not only an IT issue

■ Increased use of management requirements in the delivery of successful sourcing

Security

This COE aims to transparently secure the enterprise without delaying new initiatives. It protects corporate assets, balances security investments with risks to business, and enforces security policies.

Attributes	Processes
■ Area of expertise—Communicating the security policy to users and other IT constituencies ■ Binding theme—Enterprise security architecture ■ Value proposition—Enabling secure business	❒ Security monitoring ❒ Data recovery—Data/media management

Skills	Automation
❒ Understanding of risks and vulnerabilities ❒ Ability to conduct audits ❒ Experience evaluating business impact of security exposures ❒ Knowledge of platform access control ❒ Knowledge of firewalls, encryption, authentication for networks ❒ Experience with public key infrastructure	❒ Public key infrastructure—Entrust, VeriSign, Baltimore, GTE ❒ Single point administration—Schumann, New Dimensions ❒ Intrusion detection/scanning—ISS, Cisco ❒ Virus scanning—Network Associates, Symantec, TrendMicro ❒ Single sign-on—Groupe Bull, Security Dynamics, Axent ❒ Firewalls—Checkpoint, Cisco

Best Practices

❏ Procedures to secure new business initiatives/applications systematically

❏ Low frequency of successful attacks/security incidents

❏ Automated user authentication and access administration

❏ Extensive deployment of single sign-on technology

❏ Reuse of security infrastructure

❏ Integration of public key infrastructure and directory technologies

❏ Prudent use of outsourcers

Metrics

❏ Security incidents/year

❏ Mean time to resolution

❏ Number (or percentage) of people with high-level authority

❏ Percentage of applications tied into a consolidated user directory

❏ Average time for handling security-related service requests, by request type

❏ Number of security administrators/users

❏ Security cost/user

❏ Percentage of security costs out of overall application/project

Futures

■ New metrics, such as security $/customer

■ New technologies to secure Web servers, middleware, consolidated storage

■ Broader use of public key

■ infrastructure

■ Selective use of biometrics for authentication

■ Selective outsourcing and out-tasking to third-party security providers

Appendix **A**

Further Reading

The following sources either were referenced in this book or are recommended as useful supplementary material.

The Adaptive Enterprise: IT Strategies to Manage Change and Enable Growth, Robertson, Bruce and Valentin Sribar, 2002. Boston, MA: Addison-Wesley. ISBN 0-201-76736-8.

Benchmarking, McNair, C. J. and Kathleen Leibfried, 1992. Essex Junction, VT: Omneo Books. ISBN 0-939246-53-8.

Best Practices: Building Your Business with Customer-Focused Solutions, Hiebler, R., Kelly, Thomas B., and Charles Ketterman, 1998. New York: Touchstone Books. ISBN 0-684-84-804-X.

Securing Business Information: Strategies to Protect the Enterprise and Its Network, Byrnes, F. Christian and Dale Kutnick, 2002. Boston, MA: Addison-Wesley. ISBN 0-201-76735-X.

Capability Maturity Model's (CMM) home page at Carnegie Mellon University's Software Engineering Institute (SEI):
   www.sei.cmu.edu/cmm/cmm.html

Glossary

ADLC *See* application development lifecycle.

application development lifecycle The complete cycle of activities involved in the development of applications.

application service provider A company to which the running of an application is outsourced. Similar in concept to the service bureau.

ASP *See* application service provider.

baseline The current status of an IT organization's operations as captured in a document or inventory.

BRM *See* business relationship management.

business relationship management Management of the relationship between a business and a group of its customers. In IT, the relationship is frequently between the IT department and its customers, the users at various LOBs.

capability maturity model A model that describes the level of maturity of the software-development process at a specific site using a scale from 1 (initial) to 5 (optimized).

cost-recovery model The model chosen by an IT organization to charge the company or the users for the services provided to them.

center of excellence   A set of related processes grouped together for better management and operational efficiency.

CMM   *See* capability maturity model.

COE   *See* center of excellence.

gap analysis   Process of finding gaps between the current state (known as the baseline) and the desired state (known as the target) of IT operations or processes.

Global 2000   The 2000 largest companies on the planet.

integration point   Places where a given process touches or intersects with other processes.

line of business   A set of related activities that form a core part of a company's business, such as manufacturing, accounting, and the like.

LOB   *See* line of business.

mean time to resolution   The average amount of time it takes an organization to resolve a problem. This number is an important metric in problem management.

metric   A quantitative measure of a process or thing.

millions of instructions per second   A measure of computational ability or capacity generally applied to mainframes.

MIPS   *See* millions of instructions per second.

modified IT metric   A metric that combines elements from pure IT metrics and business metrics (which the end-user would employ).

MTTR   *See* mean time to resolution.

operations   The collection of tasks and processes traditonally involved in running a company's computing infrastructure.

PMM   *See* process maturity modeling.

process   A collection of one or more related tasks as performed at a given company.

process maturity modeling   A system of rating the maturity of processes, using a scale from 1 (immature) to 5 (mature). It is inspired by the Capability Maturity Model.

rapid response team   A team of skilled individuals, generally part of a COE, who handle changes in operations quickly and efficiently.

relationship manager   An IT employee who performs BRM functions by serving as a liaison between IT and a LOB.

RM   *See* relationship manager.

RRT   *See* rapid response team.

service-level agreement   An agreement that states at what level a service—such as Internet uptime, for example—will be provided. Failure to maintain the agreed level results in specified penalties, generally financial.

shareholder value added   A measure of value added to shareholder equity.

SLA *See* service-level agreement.

SVA *See* shareholder value added.

target   The desired quality state toward which a company is migrating. Targets are important aspects of gap analysis.

task   A piece of work that is generally performed for one purpose by one individual. Tasks may have subtasks, which are smaller units of work. Tasks are aggregated into processes.

time and materials   A basis for pricing in which a provider charges based on the actual time and materials used on a project, contrasted with fixed price.

Index